$200

$300

CAROLYN AMBUTER'S
NEEDLEPOINT CELEBRATIONS

CAROLYN AMBUTER'S NEEDLEPOINT CELEBRATIONS

ILLUSTRATIONS BY PATTI BAKER RUSSELL
PHOTOGRAPHS BY JERRY DARVIN

WORKMAN PUBLISHING COMPANY
QUADRANGLE/THE NEW YORK TIMES BOOK CO.
NEW YORK

Published in association with
Workman Publishing Company, Inc.

Copyright © 1976 by Carolyn Ambuter. All rights reserved.
No portion of this book may be reproduced—
mechanically, electronically or by any other means,
including photocopying—without written permission from
Workman Publishing Company,
231 East 51 Street, New York, New York 10022.

Hardcover edition published simultaneously in Canada
by Fitzhenry & Whiteside, Ltd., Toronto

Library of Congress Cataloging in Publication Data

Ambuter, Carolyn.
Carolyn Ambuter's needlepoint celebrations.

Bibliography: p.
1. Canvas embroidery—Patterns. I. Title:
Needlepoint celebrations.
TT778.C3A49   746.4'4   75-8305
ISBN 0-8129-0583-0

Jacket and book design: Paul Hanson
Manufactured in the United States of America
First printing
12345678910

To Joseph Ambuter

ACKNOWLEDGMENTS

From its very conception, *Needlepoint Celebrations* was to have all-new designs of lasting quality, and they were to be stitched and mounted as finished items. This was an ambitious project. To research the ideas and plan the designs were tasks of great pleasure and satisfaction. To put the designs on canvas took skill and experience because their eventual use by the reader had to be kept continually in mind. My warm appreciation goes to Patti Baker Russell and Sherry Gordon for their help in the undertaking of this artwork, which was carried out with their usual faithfulness and thoroughness.

Then came the realization that there were sixty-one items to be worked. Here I must give my most heartfelt and sincere thanks to the gracious people who stitched with such love and care the canvases that were planned for them and about them.

Martha Sears Barclay (Mrs. Frederick Beale Barclay): *Pennsylvania German Fractur Birth Record* and *Capricorn Pillow*

Anne Cromwell (Mrs. Roger J.K. Cromwell): *Zodiac Rug* and *Leo Pillow*

Mel Davis (Mrs. Kenneth E. Davis): *Aquarius Picture*

Dianna E. Dawkins (Mrs. Thomas Dawkins): *May Pillow*

Meme Ferree (Mrs. Edward Ferree): *December Pillow*

Sue Fiordelisi (Mrs. N. Fiordelisi), Sue's Needlepoint, New York City: *October Pillow*

Sherry Gordon: *Provincial Birth Record*

Catherine Jackson (Mrs. Robert Scott Jackson), Middle Gallery, Massachusetts: *Taurus Pillow, Open and Closed Sign,* and *Shop Sign*

Ethel Jay (Mrs. Byron Jay): *April Pillow* and *July Pillow*

Virginia S. Mailman (Mrs. Norton Mailman): *Chinoiserie Anniversary Pillow*

Mary Moskow (Mrs. Nathan Moskow): *Cancer or the Moonchild Pillow*

Janet Ann Packer (Mrs. John W. Packer, Jr.): *Capricorn, Aquarius, Gemini,* and *Cancer symbols* and *ABC Appliqué Quilt*

Claire Putnam (Mrs. Charlton D. Putnam): *Taurus Pillow*

Doris Rindler (Mrs. Alfred G. Rindler): *January Pillow*

Linda Baker Russell (daughter of Patti Baker Russell and Donald F. Russell): *Virgo Pillow*

Norma Yarkovsky (Mrs. Alfred Yarkovsky), Kate's Trade Shop, New York City: *February Plaque, March Plaque, November Plaque* and *Twelve Days of Christmas Sock*

And I want to thank Patti Baker Russell very specially for her cooperation and her gorgeous, meticulous artwork and for stitching the following items: *June Plaque, Libra Picture, Aries, Leo, & Libra symbols, American Eagle Pillow, Clock Pillow,* and *Horn of Plenty Picture*

In addition, for encouragement and care, thank you to Peter Workman, my co-publisher, to Sally Kovalchick and Patricia Murray, my editors, and my daughter Jean Harris for her literary encouragement.

CONTENTS

INTRODUCTION 15

SPECIAL OCCASIONS 19

TIME 41

FOR OUR CHILDREN 111

SPECIAL INTERESTS 133

MATERIALS AND HOW TO START AND FINISH 171

STITCHES AND STITCH VOCABULARY 183

LETTERING AND ALPHABETS 205

APPENDIX 217

INTRODUCTION

The surge of interest in needlepoint that has been gaining momentum during this second half of the twentieth century can be compared with a similar rage for needlework during the early nineteenth century. At that time, rural Americans had managed to satisfy their basic needs (warmth, food, and clothing). For the first time, women could dress up their homes and follow fads in fancywork. They quilted both patchwork and appliqué bed coverings, hooked rugs, and embroidered pictures.

Today, most of America is thoroughly mechanized, and our relatively new leisure time has afforded us the extreme luxury of making by hand articles that could be made more economically by machine.

Needlepoint is one of the most satisfying of the needle arts. Like weaving, it involves making a fabric, rather than decorating a surface. The quiet, constant repetition of stitching both calms and excites the worker, who experiences the pleasure of watching a richly textured design emerge from a flimsy netting. It is very difficult to fret and worry once you are absorbed in a rewarding piece of needlepoint.

Therapeutic though it may be, needlepoint is above all an *artistic* activity. Artistic merit is the chief reason for displaying needlepoint. If therapy is to be its only purpose, the project should be kept in a closet, not put in a place of importance. We ought to select designs and projects that stand on their own artistically and do not clutter our surroundings with meaningless and unenduring trivia.

Needlepoint Celebrations is intended to stimulate the creation of projects of meaning and taste. If there is an important event in your life or in the life of someone dear to you, why not commemorate it with a gift of your handiwork, your time, and your care in planning its composition and significance? With needlepoint as a tool, you can draw inspiration from art history, record your life and interests and those of your family, and incorporate in your work the colors and spirit of today.

The projects in this book are divided into four categories. "Special Occasions" suggests ways to commemorate all the happy, historical events in our lives: births, graduations, marriages, new homes, and anniversaries.

"Time" shows how to employ design devices—a "Calendar of Flowers," the signs and symbols of astrology, a clockface—to create highly personal works that celebrate birthdays, anniversaries, and other important events.

"For Our Children" is dedicated to the creation of needlepoint worthy of passage from one generation to the next. It provides methods of recording your personal history, wishes, love, and joy with stitches.

"Special Interests" offers ways to incorporate hobbies, professions, leisure interests, and trades into very individual needlepoint creations.

Needlepoint Celebrations also contains sections on methods and techniques. "Materials and How to Start and Finish" includes a description of various kinds of canvases, types of yarns, sizes of needles, and all the additional equipment used to make these celebrations. It also explains how to paint a design on canvas, how to read the graphs, and how to finish a piece.

"Stitches and Stitch Vocabulary" is obviously a section on stitches. Because this book emphasizes design, the number of stitches has been deliberately limited. However, practical and versatile stitches, each described in detail and diagrammed, are included to provide you with a useful and interesting stitch vocabulary.

"Lettering and Alphabets" includes graphs of the many alphabets used in the designs in this book. It is an especially important section because almost all the projects contain some message, inscription, dedication, or documentation. The text introduction explains how to plan and position lettering using graphs.

In addition, there is a "Color Chart" listing all the yarn colors used in the original works in case you wish to duplicate them. It should be used in conjunction with the color photographs.

It is my hope that *Needlepoint Celebrations* will be used as a workbook and that, in addition to recreating the specific projects, you will use the book as a point of departure. A motif from one design might be combined with an element from another pattern, or it might be used by itself. A pillow might be transformed into a chair seat or a picture. Mix and match motifs. Here are the tools. Use them, enjoy them, and celebrate life with them.

Carolyn Ambuter

SPECIAL OCCASIONS

A child is born; an anniversary is celebrated; a daughter is wed; a friend becomes engaged; a new home is acquired; a grandchild is graduated. These are great events in our lives and the lives of the people we love. You may decide that the warmest, happiest way to commemorate such a special occasion is to record it permanently in a very personal piece of needlepoint. By giving careful attention to the selection of an appropriate design, an inscription, and decorative stitches, you will create a valued family heirloom that will give pleasure throughout the years to come.

CHINOISERIE ANNIVERSARY PILLOW

(SEE PAGE 27)

Today, we think of China as a serious, industrious nation with a uniformed, well-fed population working on its huge communal farms and in its factories in an atmosphere of pleasant countryside and bustling cities. But from the days of Marco Polo's first revelations in the thirteenth century until the end of the eighteenth century, the Western world fantasized a Chinese utopia in which ritual and leisure were the main occupations. During the 1700s, poets, painters, and philosophers turned to the East for inspiration. Pictures of their fantasies, called *chinoiserie*, bear little resemblance to the art of China; they are European conceptions — idealizations, really — of Chinese conduct and manners.

The chinoiserie world is a land of snowcapped mountains surrounding garden vignettes. It is a country of perpetual spring, where painted, latticed garden houses have jingling bells dangling from their turned-up corners, and where porcelain pagodas nestle among the trees. Delicate junks and dragon boats float past riverbanks covered with weeping willows. Chrysanthemums and peonies tower over tiny, doll-like people fishing and writing poetry. Adorable, round-faced children play games with porcelain balls or fly marvelous kites, and courtiers and their ladies enjoy each other's company.

In this chinoiserie pillow, which was stitched in celebration of a tenth wedding anniversary, a pagodalike summerhouse is surrounded with foliage, peonies and bamboo tower over the temple, enormous butterflies hover about, and a couple sits quietly, enjoying the tinkling of the bells. A *treillage* (a kind of latticework) encloses this pastoral scene and provides space for a personal inscription. In the center opening of the fretwork, the stitcher entered her marriage date; in the openings to the left and the right, she stitched her own and her husband's initials respectively. The colors used in the design are typical chinoiserie porcelain colors. The two greens of the background and the treillage were selected to harmonize with a light green treillage-patterned bed cover.

The treillage could be used alone to frame a stitched message or a monogram; the scene might make a smaller cushion or a chair seat. Stitched on a 10-mesh canvas, this design would make a striking bench or ottoman cover; on a larger mesh (5 or 7 to the inch), a small hearth or bedside rug.

ENDLESS KNOT WEDDING PICTURE

(SEE PAGE 30)

This framed piece of needlepoint was designed and stitched as a family record of marriage to be enjoyed both as a picture and as an endless celebration. It was inspired by a type of eighteenth-century American valentine called a *truelove knot* or an *endless knot of love*. These valentines were hand drawn and colored, sometimes in red and blue, so that the colors formed a complex maze (or endless knot) of heart shapes. The bands of the knot were carefully inscribed with messages of love.

In this simplified love knot design, the name of the bride is entered on the left, the name of the groom on the right, and the wedding date in the middle as a reminder of celebrations to come. To stitch an "Endless Knot Wedding Picture" is to create a permanent record of your love and best wishes.

The endless knot design might make a pillow, a tray, or a tabletop. The picture can be enlarged with additional bands of ribbon. And, of course, another commemorative message could be used.

GOOD LUCK PILLOW

(SEE PAGE 32)

One leaf for fame,
And one for wealth,
One for a faithful lover,
And one to bring you glorious health
Are in a four-leaf clover.

Mattioli's *Commentaires* (Lyons, 1597)

During the eighteenth and nineteenth centuries, a very poetic *language of flowers* was used by lovers. This flowery symbolism came from ancient Persia, but it was introduced into Europe by Charles II of Sweden, who spent five years exiled in Turkey. Every flower represented a human meaning. The four-leaf clover's message is "be mine." Today, in the tradition of the Celts, the Druids, and the ancient Greeks, we think of the four-leaf clover as a good luck charm.

This little pillow might be made as a good luck token in honor of a special occasion: a graduation, a new job, a retirement. And because of its flowery sentiment, it would also make a lovely engagement present.

ROSE SCROLL MEMORY BOOK

(SEE PAGE 34)

This handsome needlepoint-and-leather loose-leaf album should be prominently displayed on a table or desk. The simple expression on the theorem scroll hints at the album's contents; its plastic envelope pages hold photographs, invitations, announcements, and treasured documents.

The rose scroll design is taken from a form of stencil painting called *theorem work,* which was popular in America in the 1800s. Theorem paintings are easily recognized by the distinct outlines of each shape and the careful blending of the colors within it. A painting was assembled by combining separate theorems, such as fruit, flowers, bowls, baskets, and other still life objects. It is easy to understand why so many paintings done in this period look so much alike. Theorems could be cut from oiled paper at home, but the designs and instructions for their use were usually sold in books. A proper young lady learned theorem work in female seminaries, and her education was considered complete only after she had received instruction in drawing, painting, and needlework.

This design can be adapted to make a pillow or a picture, with a different short message, a monogram, or the date of a birth, a graduation, or a wedding stitched within the scroll.

BLESS THIS HOUSE HANGING

(SEE PAGE 36)

Many symbolic good wishes are interwoven in the design of this stitched house gift. The horseshoe is a symbol of good fortune and has been regarded as such for as long as horses have worn shoes. According to tradition, when the shoe is nailed in place, it acts as a charm to prevent the good fortune from traveling. The horseshoe should always be hung with the opening at the top; this will keep the good luck from spilling. To live "in clover" means to live in very pleasant and prosperous circumstances. Little wonder. This wild plant, which can be found along any roadside in North America, contributes nitrogen to the soil and is often planted with hay in dairy country and with grass in lawns. It is also a valuable source of nectar for honey bees. In fact, clover was one of the earliest plants to be cultivated for its agricultural value. The Romans used a bundle of wheat to denote power. Wheat is called the *staff of life,* and it is the principal ingredient of "our daily bread."

All these good wishes are tied with a delicate blue bow and inscribed with a blessing. You might also want to embroider the name of the homeowner within the horseshoe. In this hanging, the stitcher used the house name *Mingean,* the Japanese word for a simple country cottage.

This design would make a stunning cover for a bench; on a larger canvas, it would make a handsome small rug.

PENNSYLVANIA GERMAN FRACTUR BIRTH RECORD

(SEE PAGE 38)

This birth record is inspired by a folk art form that originated with the German settlers who sought religious freedom in Pennsylvania during colonial times. *Fractur,* which is the name that was given to this type of painting by the Pennsylvanians, combines primitively drawn designs of fanciful birds, flowers, and sometimes biblical figures with a jagged form of writing derived from German or Gothic lettering. Until the introduction of the English school system in 1850, Pennsylvania community schools instructed children in the art of religious fractur. The children decorated passages from the Bible and moral precepts with alphabets and fractur designs. Needy ministers frequently supplemented their incomes by preparing *presentation pieces,* documents commemorating births, baptisms, betrothals, deaths. Itinerant fractur artists prepared paintings in advance and added the lettering to order. Birth records were by far the most popular.

This design uses the original colors found in old fracturs and sets them off on a natural background.

Chinoiserie Anniversary Pillow

Canvas: 14-mesh mono

Yarn: 4-ply wool twist for white and dark green backgrounds; 7-ply silk for all other colors

Stitches: Tent; border outside treillage, Continuous Mosaic

Finishing: 13½ by 24½ inches, backed and boxed with green moiré

Endless Knot
Wedding Picture

Canvas: 10/20-mesh Penelope

Yarn: silk

Stitches: knot, Cross; flowers, Petit Point (3 ply); lettering, petit Slanted Gobelin (4 ply) over Petit Point (4 ply); background, diagonal Rep

Finishing: 13⅞ by 14 inches, mounted on a stretcher

Good Luck Pillow

Canvas: 14-mesh mono

Yarn: rose, Persian; greens, wool twist

Stitches: rose background, Continuous Mosaic (2 ply); pink outlines, Slanted Gobelin (over two threads); Asterisk (2 ply); clover, lettering, and green background and flaps, Tent

Finishing: 12½ by 12 inches; needlepoint flaps for boxing, 1 inch; backing, rose velvet

Rose Scroll
Memory Book

Canvas: 14-mesh mono

Yarn: Persian

Stitches: design, Tent (2 ply); accents on lettering, Crossed Mosaic; background, horizontal rib Diagonal Rep

Finishing: exposed needlepoint, 11½ by 9½ inches (check with mounter for exact size of finished piece); finished album, 12 by 10 inches; pages, 11 by 9 inches; binding, pink leather; lining, pink moiré

Bless This House Hanging

Canvas: 10-mesh mono

Yarn: Persian

Stitches: Tent; border, Cushion

Finishing: 16¾ by 21¾ inches, mounted on a stretcher

***Pennsylvania
German Fractur
Birth Record***

Canvas: 14-mesh mono

Yarn: Persian

Stitches: Tent; accents on lettering, Slanted Gobelin

Finishing: 14 by 15 inches, mounted on a stretcher

TIME

CALENDAR OF FLOWERS

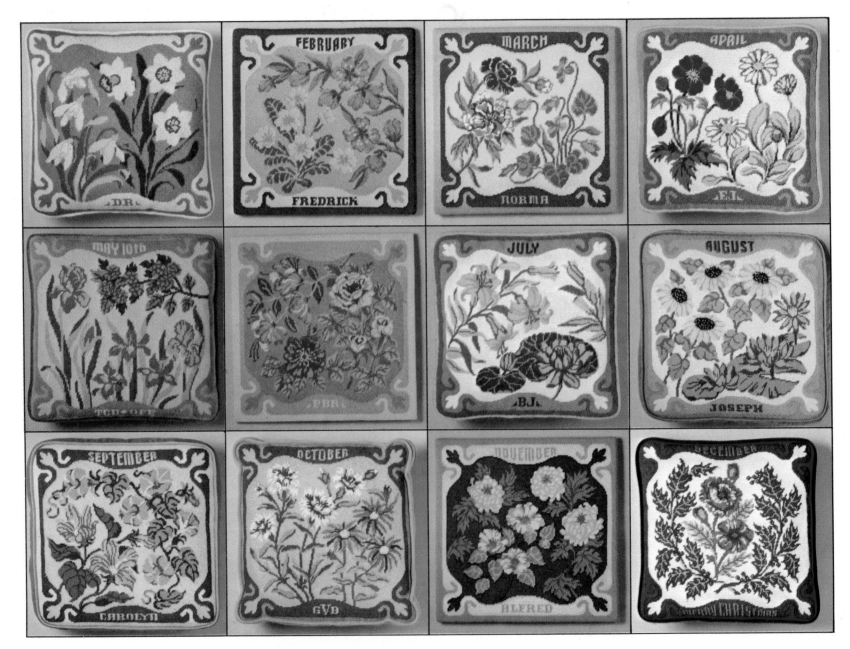

THE LANGUAGE AND SYMBOLISM OF A CALENDAR OF FLOWERS

Throughout history, flowers have been a subject of endless fascination. They figure prominently in the world's heritage of religious and mythological symbolism. Think of the chaste lily, symbol of resurrection, and of the sacred lotus, emblem of past, present, and future. Man has marked the passage of time according to their growing seasons. The Chinese have a flower calendar; the Japanese, flowers of the months. The flirtatious and sentimental "language of flowers" so popular in the Western world during the eighteenth century was derived from ancient Persian lore. Most of all, people have always celebrated the joy and beauty of life by surrounding themselves with flowers.

These "Calendar of Flowers" designs have been adapted from the Chinese, Japanese, and English calendars of flowers, with a few additions based on American traditions. Each composition features a pair of flowers appropriate to a specific month. But the designs are perfect for mixing and matching. Any of these pairings might be changed, depending on the whim of the stitcher, or a single flower might be used in another design. The art nouveau border that surrounds these floral pillows and plaques might be used to frame a pertinent message, a monogram, or an entirely different design.

A complete set of pillows offers many decorative possibilities. Six of them could be displayed on a sofa for half a year and then replaced by the other six, according to the appropriate seasons. A wall of floral plaques would be stunning, particularly in a room that is filled with houseplants.

A traceable drawing that can be transferred onto canvas is provided for each floral composition. And each drawing is accompanied by the symbolism of the "Calendar of Flowers" to add to the stitcher's enjoyment in working the design. The border used for all twelve designs is carefully graphed to ensure accurate stitching. The top and bottom sections of the border are roomy enough to accommodate names, dates, initials, or whatever suits the stitcher's purpose. (The lettering used in these designs can be found on page 214.)

All the "Calendar of Flowers" pillows and plaques were worked on 12-mesh German mono canvas with 2-ply Persian yarn. The finished pieces measured 13½ to 14½ inches square. Extra rows of stitches were added in most cases for seam allowance, turn back, and turn under. (See "Materials and How to Start and Finish.")

A horticulturist, gardener, or flower fancier might like to make the complete "Calendar of Flowers" with matching borders. The backgrounds could all be the same color but changed in depth according to the season. A rug of flowers is another possibility; it would have the additional interest of a secondary pattern formed by the borders at the points where four squares meet. These designs would also make beautiful covers for dining room chairs, especially if more background is added outside the border to set off the entire composition. By using a smaller or larger mesh and changing the ply of the yarn, these designs could be adapted to make coasters (omitting the borders), handbags, or book or album covers (what a beautiful way to cover a lowly telephone directory). Give your imagination free rein; the possibilities are endless.

JANUARY PILLOW:
SNOWDROP AND DAFFODIL

(SEE PAGE 50)

The "January Pillow" is unmarked at the top because it was stitched by a gardener who particularly enjoys snowdrops and daffodils. Only her initials are worked in the lower border. It is mounted as a knife-edged sofa pillow and backed with off-white cotton velvet. The gentle coloring is suitable for even the most formal room.

FEBRUARY PLAQUE:
PRIMROSE AND PEACHBLOSSOM

(SEE PAGE 52)

The "February Plaque" is one of a set of flower pictures that also includes March and November. These pictures were made to hang on a bedroom wall that is covered with a collection of needlepoint pictures. The birth months of the family members are stitched in the top borders, and their first names are entered at the bottoms. The colors were chosen to match and harmonize with the room's color scheme.

MARCH PLAQUE:
VIOLET AND TREE PEONY

(SEE PAGE 54)

March is printed at the top of this picture. The name of the birthday girl appears in the bottom border. It is one of a group of three plaques that use the same three colors in different arrangements for the backgrounds (see "February Plaque" and "November Plaque"). The background color of one becomes a border color of another. However, a more closely matched set might be stitched using the same color placement for all three borders and backgrounds.

APRIL PILLOW: DAISY AND ANEMONE

(SEE PAGE 56)

The "April Pillow" is one of a pair. (Its mate is the "July Pillow.") The pillows celebrate the birth months of a husband and wife, and their initials were stitched in the lower borders. These pillows were mounted as 14-inch-square box pillows and backed with gold velvet to match the gold yarn used in the designs.

MAY PILLOW: HAWTHORN AND IRIS

(SEE PAGE 58)

The "May Pillow" is marked at the top with a marriage anniversary date and at the bottom with a pair of initials. It is mounted with a knife edge and backed with a soft rose velvet that matches the yarn used for the hawthorns. The design's delicate colors give the pillow a rich brocade quality. The overall effect is elegant and quite formal.

JUNE PLAQUE: HONEYSUCKLE AND ROSE

(SEE PAGE 60)

June's delicate flowers were stitched as a plaque to be hung in a bedroom. Only the initials of the needleworker were entered in the lower border. The white in the border creates a matlike effect.

JULY PILLOW: LILY AND WATER LILY

(SEE PAGE 62)

The "July Pillow" is the companion to the "April Pillow." Fresh as country chintz watercolors, they make a very cheerful pair and are used propped at the heads of twin beds. The same color palette is used for both pillows, but the border colors are reversed to make a lively contrast.

AUGUST PILLOW: SUNFLOWER AND LOTUS

(SEE PAGE 64)

The "August Pillow" commemorates a birth date with the name of the month in the top border and the name of the birthday person in the lower border. This is half of another pair of box pillows. (September is the other.) Both the month and the name were stitched in Tent and then overstitched with Slanted Gobelin. The pink lotus matches the pink mallows in the "September Pillow."

SEPTEMBER PILLOW: MALLOW AND MORNING GLORY

(SEE PAGE 66)

The colors used for the "September Pillow" are coordinated with those used for the "August Pillow." And the month and name are stitched to match (Tent overstitched with Slanted Gobelin). Designed to be used in a highly personal room, they are colorful and lively and are backed with gold velvet to match the color of the dust ruffles of the beds they adorn.

OCTOBER PILLOW:
CARNATION AND ASTER

(SEE PAGE 68)

The "October Pillow" also honors a birth month and was a gift from the stitcher to her sister, whose monogram it bears. It is made with scalloped corners and is boxed; the velvet backing matches the gold yarn of the background. The dark, rich colors of this autumn floral design blend with the living room in which it is displayed.

NOVEMBER PLAQUE:
CHRYSANTHEMUM AND CAMELLIA

(SEE PAGE 70)

The "November Plaque" is the third in the family group (along with the "February" and "March" plaques) and also bears the names of the month and the birthday celebrant. Extra rows of stitching were made for the side returns of these plaques. (See "Materials and How to Start and Finish" for details on making an unframed picture.) The colors are bright and cheerful and match those of the room in which the trio hangs.

DECEMBER PILLOW:
HOLLY AND POPPY

(SEE PAGE 72)

December is the Christmas month, and so it is represented in this pillow with a wreathlike design of holly and poppies and a holiday greeting stitched in the lower border. This pillow can be put away when the tree is taken down and then brought out again to brighten the next Christmas season, establishing a pleasant holiday tradition.

January Pillow

Snowdrop (from an English calendar): hope and consolation, emblem of early spring

Daffodil (from an American tradition): regard, emblem of the Annunciation, flower of Easter

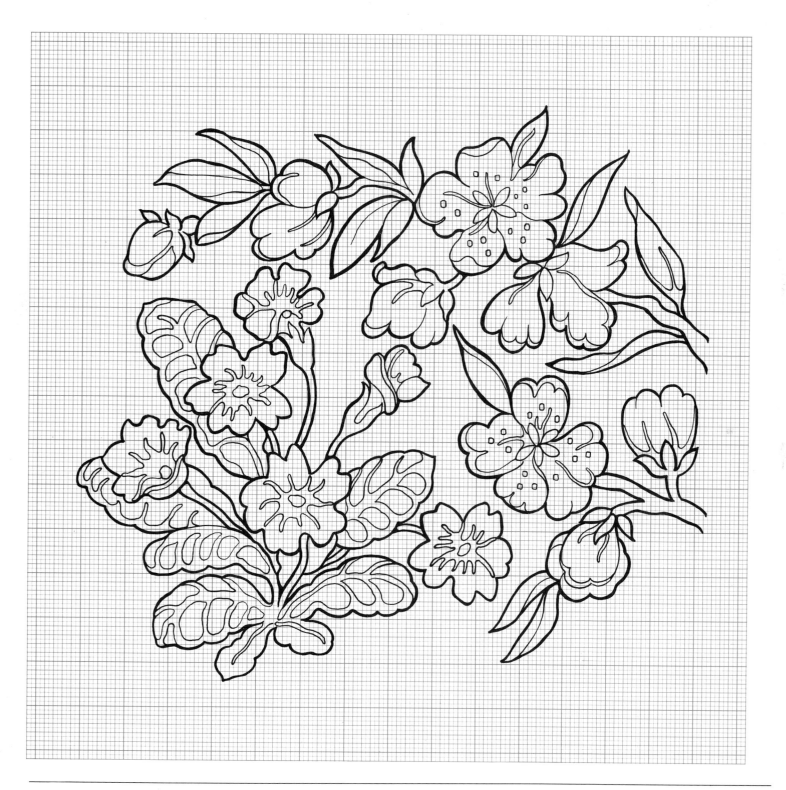

February Plaque

Primrose (from an English calendar): early youth and young love, "I am your captive."

Peachblossom (from the Chinese calendar): bridal hope and generosity, symbol of longevity and marriage

March Plaque

Tree Peony (from the Chinese calendar): symbol of love and affection, emblem of spring

Violet (from an English calendar): modesty and simplicity, good luck gift to a woman, "I return your love!"

April Pillow

Anemone (from an American tradition): refusal and abandonment, forsaken, a herald of spring

Daisy (from an English calendar): gentleness and innocence, purity in thought and loyal love

May Pillow

Hawthorn (from an English calendar): sweet hope and marriage, "You are my only queen!"

Iris (from the Japanese calendar): faith, wisdom, and valor; hope, light, and power

June Plaque

Honeysuckle (from an English calendar): devotion and affection, generosity and gaiety, bond of love, "We belong to each other!"

Rose (from an American tradition): charm and innocence, symbol of secrecy and silence, "You are so pure and lovely!"

July Pillow

Lily (from an American tradition): sincerity and majesty, purity, chastity, and innocence

Water Lily (from an English calendar): eloquence and persuasion, purity of heart

August Pillow

Sunflower (from an American tradition): homage and devotion, symbol of the sun, "My eyes see only you!"

Lotus (from an American tradition): mystery and truth, symbol of the sun, golden throne of Buddha, flower of midsummer

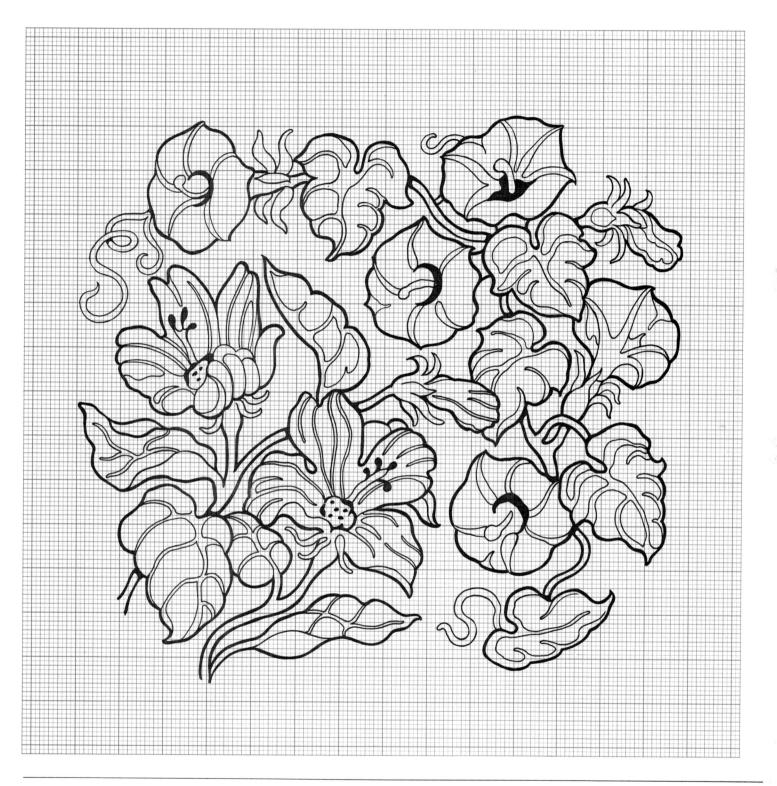

September Pillow

Mallow (from the Chinese calendar): magic charm against evil spirits, delicate beauty and gentle affection, maternal tenderness and beneficence

Morning Glory (from an English calendar): farewell and departure, symbol of mortality

October Pillow

Carnation (from an American tradition): pure and ardent love, admiration and worldly sentiments, "Alas for my poor heart!"

Aster (from an American tradition): elegance and daintiness, talisman of love, herb of Venus

70

November Plaque

Camellia (from an American tradition): excellence and steadfastness, "I shall love you always!"

Chrysanthemum (from an English calendar): cheerfulness and optimism, rest and ease, long life and happiness

December Pillow

Holly (from an English calendar): foresight and defense, "I dare not approach!"

Poppy (from the Chinese calendar): imagination and dreaminess, emblem of evil and dissipation, consolation, fantastic extravagance

THE ASTROLOGICAL YEAR

Although most of the Western world marks time according to the Julian calendar (January to December), there is also an astrological system, in which the year begins with Aries (March 21) and ends with Pisces (March 20). This system is based on the relative positions of planets and their effects on man. Zodiac signs are assigned to points along an imaginary belt that circles the earth, and the sun rises in a different sign of the zodiac every month. Horoscopes are cast and fortunes interpreted according to the sun's position at the time of a person's birth. The position of the stars tells an astrologer much about an individual's future, health, character, and other aspects of his life.

The signs of the zodiac are a rich source of design elements because of their individual associations with colors, metals, plants, and jewels. And, of course, specific character traits are attributed to each sign. (You will find these listed in the section "Zodiac Symbols.") In the "Zodiac Rug," and in the "Leo" and "Sagittarius" pillows, some of the recipients' astrologically determined characteristics were listed along with their names and birth dates.

All twelve zodiac designs were stitched on a 10-mesh canvas with 3-ply Persian. They were planned as 12-inch-square pictures or pillows. Because the designs are uncomplicated, with large areas of solid color, they are especially suitable for beginners working in Tent. For more advanced stitchers, the designs make fine pieces for learning new stitches and combinations.

Although specific colors are traditionally assigned to each sign, liberties were taken in the coloring of these designs. In almost every case, the yarn colors were chosen to harmonize with the room that was to house the finished piece of work.

It must be said that the idea of assembling the "Zodiac Rug" was an afterthought. The original plan called for a group of six pillows, each commemorating the birth of a family member. However, as the completed pieces began to pile up, putting them together as a family Christmas present seemed to be a perfectly marvelous thing to do.

Because all the designs were worked on 10-mesh canvas, with their selvages in the same position (on the lower edge), it was possible to block the finished squares to the same size. The rug was designed to have three canvases at the top and three at the bottom, with a 1-inch navy band around each square. (Where there were common edges, a 2-inch border was formed.) The entire rug was framed with a slightly wider band of light coral, a larger band of dark coral, and a final 1-inch band of navy.

The first step in assembling the rug was to outline the position of the squares and the bands of color on a larger 10-mesh canvas (42 inches wide and 59 inches long). The selvages of the larger canvas matched the direction of the selvages of the smaller canvases. (A standard canvas 40-inches wide could have been used, but the margins for blocking would have been narrower.) Then, the selvages were removed from the blocked squares to eliminate bulk. The four corners of each square were pressed back dog-ear fashion and all raw edges were pressed to the back, leaving one row of blank canvas thread on all four sides of each square. A Long-Armed Cross was then used to attach each square to the larger canvas, using two rows of canvas threads (one from the stitched square and one from the backing canvas). The Long-Armed Cross, a traditional Portuguese rug stitch, was also used for the border bands. It is quick, easy, and does not distort. Perhaps this rug would have been simpler to make on one canvas, but working individual squares was easy and convenient. The effect of the appliqued canvases is quite charming.

Aries:
Zodiac Rug

Stitches: head, Continuous Mosaic; body, Mosaic; rump and forelegs, Cushion with Backstitch; lettering, Tent; symbol, vertical Kalem; spot, Asterisk; background, Tent

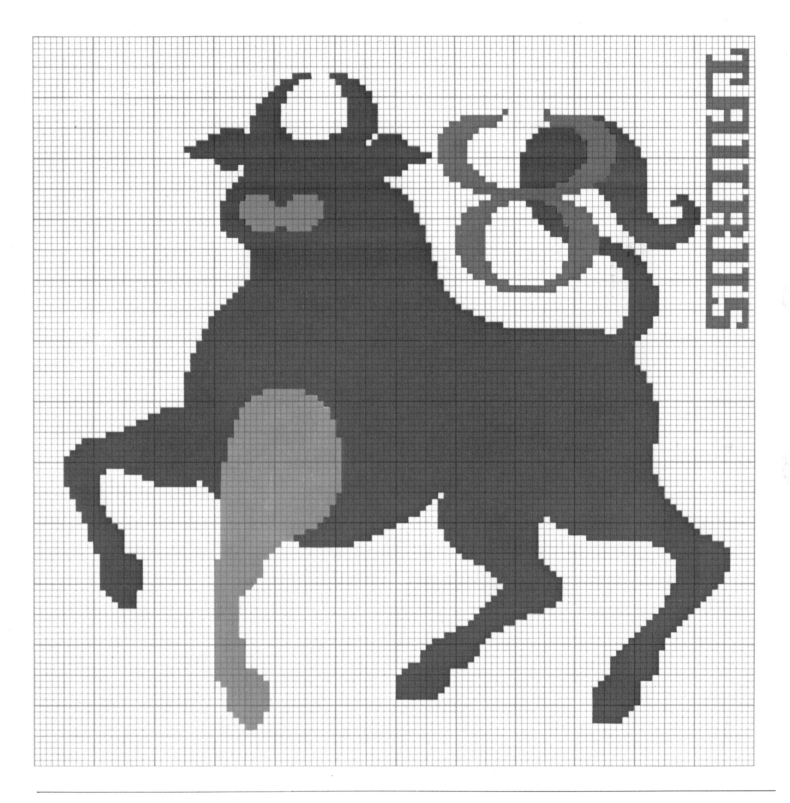

Taurus Pillow **Stitches:** "Taurus," Slanted Gobelin; body, Mosaic; mouth, foreleg, symbol, other lettering, Tent; lettering background, Tent; background, Continuous Mosaic

Gemini:
Zodiac Rug

Stitches: suits, vertical Kalem; bodies, Tent; lettering and symbol, Tent; spot, Asterisk; background, Rep

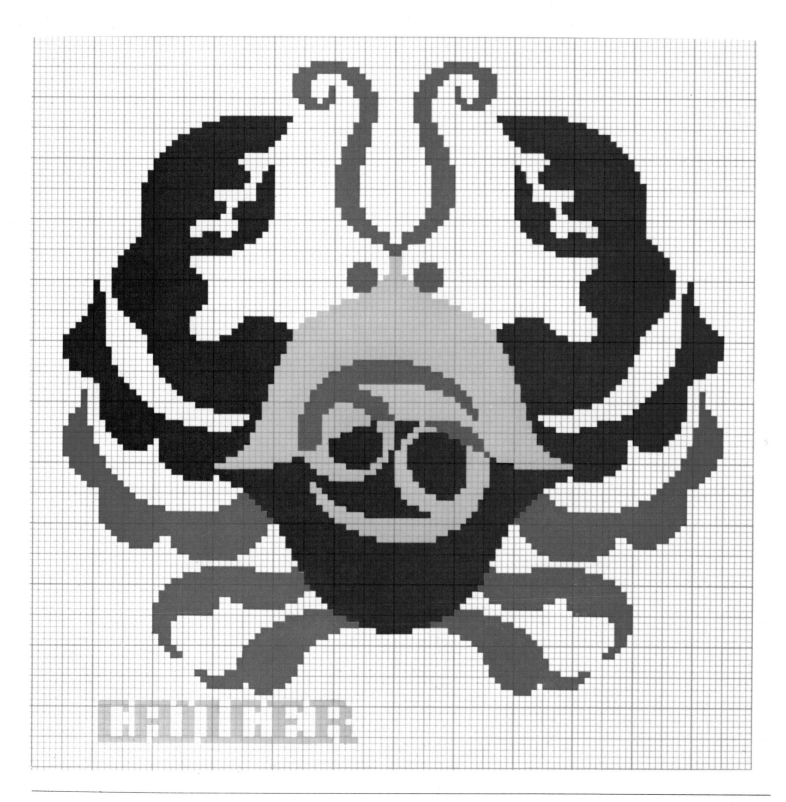

Cancer or the Moonchild Pillow

Stitches: body, Tent; eyes, Asterisk; lettering, Slanted Gobelin with Tent; lettering background, Tent; background, Rep horizontal rib

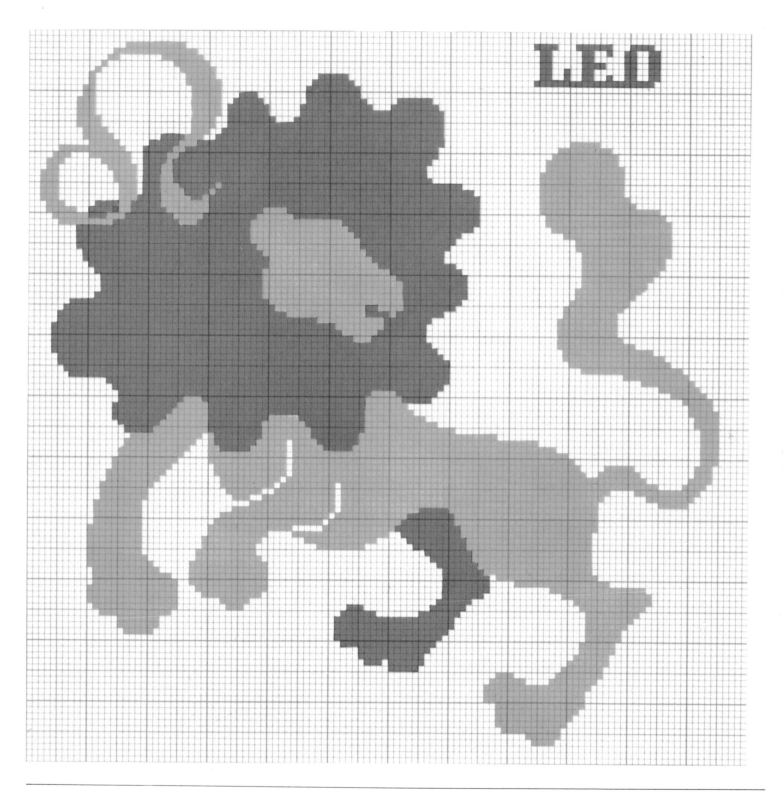

Leo Pillow

Stitches: face, Tent; mane, Mosaic with Crossed Mosaic; tail, vertical Kalem; "Leo," Slanted Gobelin; symbol and initials, Tent; spot, Asterisk; lettering background, Tent; background, Continuous Mosaic

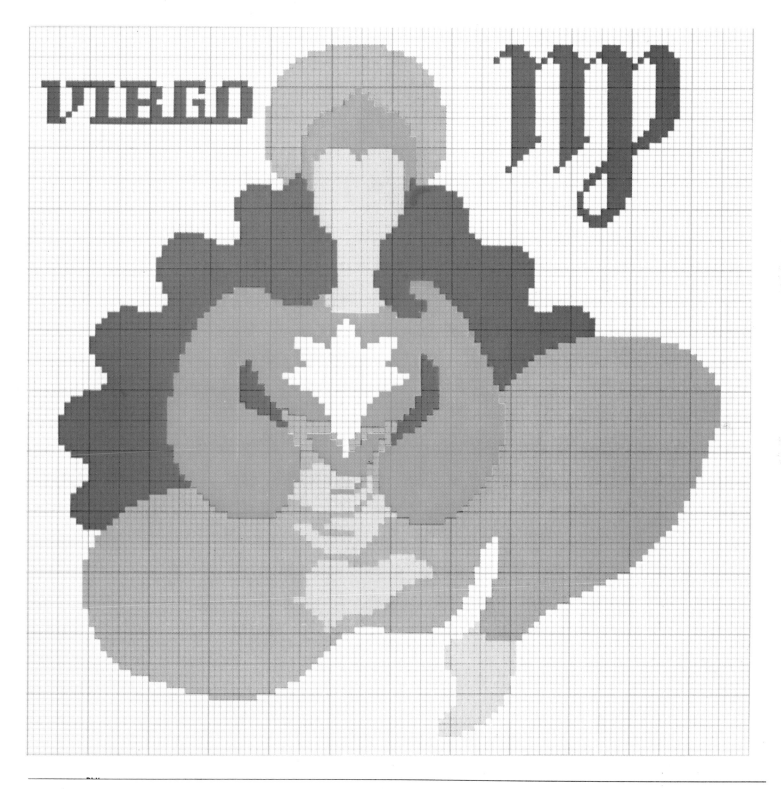

Virgo Pillow

Stitches: blouse and lily, Continuous Mosaic slanting right; trousers, Flat slanting left; body and hair, Tent slanting left; lettering and symbol, Slanted Gobelin slanting right; lettering background, Tent slanting right; background, Continuous Mosaic slanting left

Libra Picture

Stitches: scales, Flat, Slanted Gobelin, Mosaic, Tent; lettering and symbol, Slanted Gobelin; border, half Flat and half Tent boxes; background, Tent

Scorpio:
Zodiac Rug

Stitches: eyes, Asterisk; claws, Continuous Mosaic slanting right and left; small claws, Tent; chest, horizontal Kalem (two ways); body, Continuous Mosaic; tail, Mosaic Chequer, Tent; background, Tent

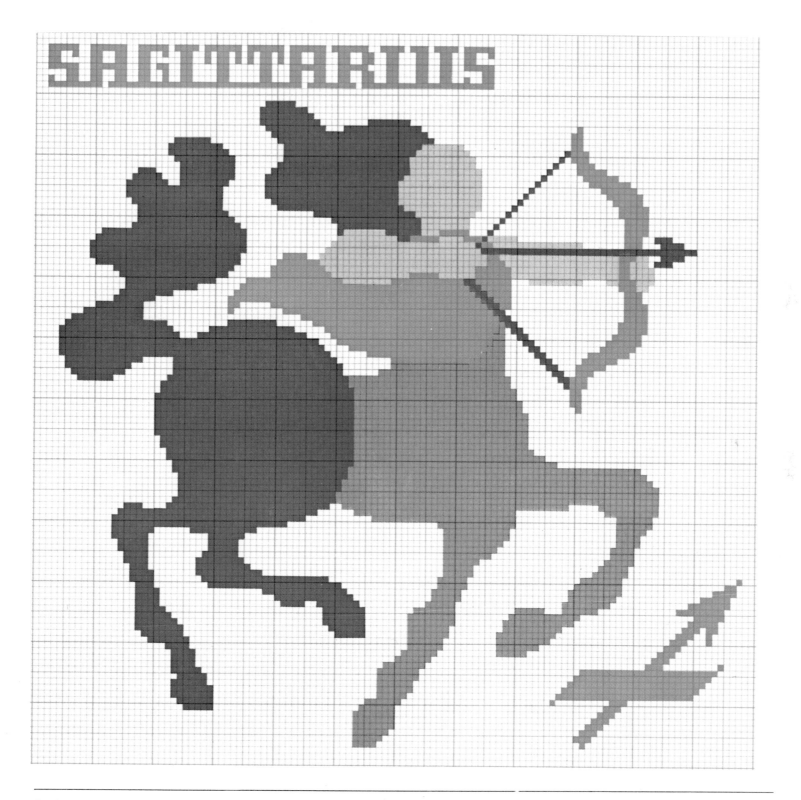

Sagittarius Pillow

Stitches: head and arm, Tent; front torso and legs, Mosaic Chequer; hind torso and legs, Mosaic and Crossed Mosaic; hair, Kalem one-way right; tail, vertical Kalem; scarf, Rep horizontal rib; bow, horizontal Kalem; arrow and bowstring, Tent; symbol, Tent; lettering, Slanted Gobelin with Tent; border, Mosaic; lettering background, Tent; background, Mosaic

Capricorn Pillow

Stitches: body, Tent; hair, Mosaic; symbol, Tent; lettering, Slanted Gobelin with Tent; lettering background, Tent; background, Continuous Mosaic

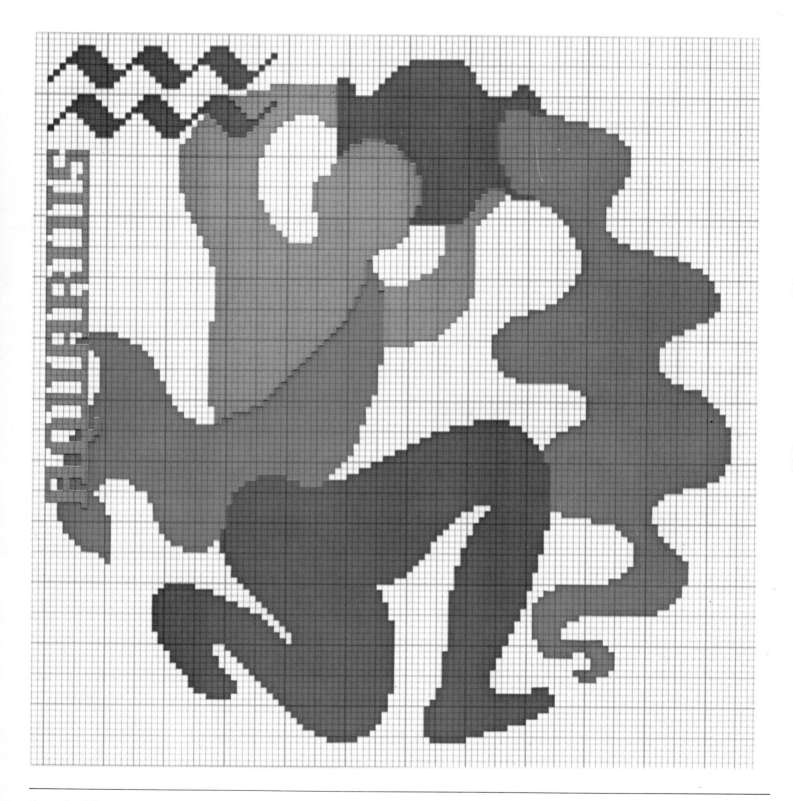

Aquarius Picture

Stitches: upper body, Tent; lower body, Continuous Cashmere; drapery, Continuous Mosaic slanting right; pitcher, Mosaic; water, Continuous Mosaic slanting left; lettering and symbol, Slanted Gobelin and Tent; background, Tent

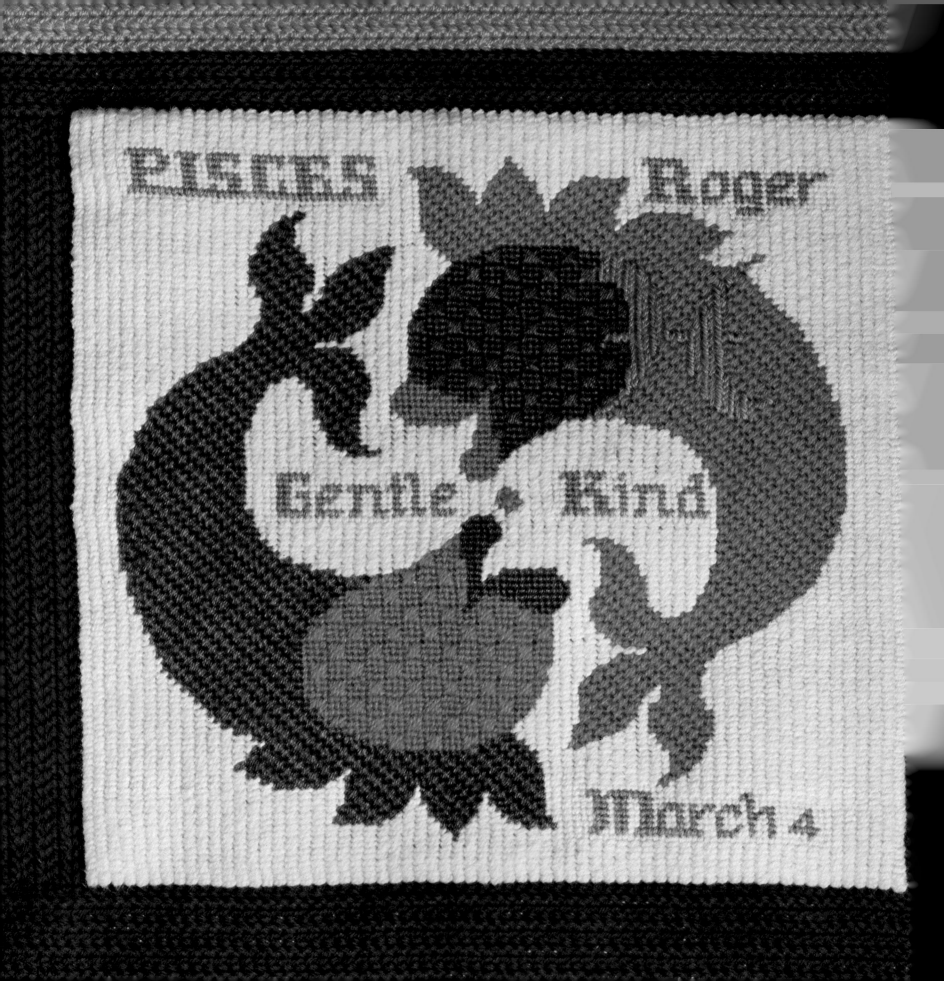

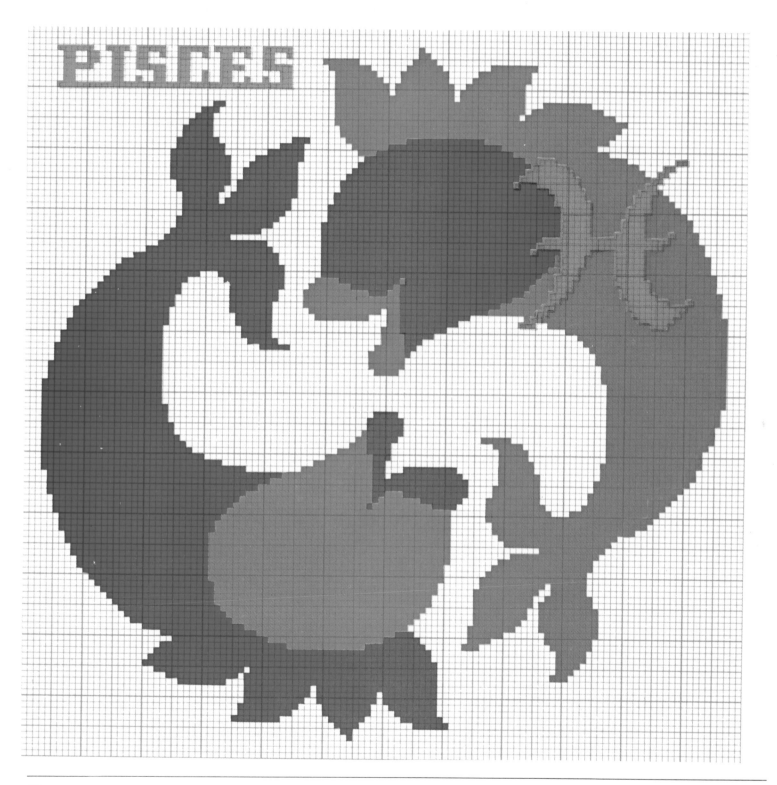

Pisces:
Zodiac Rug

Stitches: bodies, Continuous Mosaic; heads, Flat Chequer; mouths, Tent; symbol, vertical Kalem; lettering, Tent; spot, Asterisk; background, Rep

ZODIAC SYMBOLS

Each sign is governed by its own planetary ruler and assigned one of the four elements: air, earth, fire, or water. In addition, each sign has its own personality traits. It seems logical, then, to use some of this material to

make very personal and amusing needlepoint pieces to observe the birthdays of family and friends. The various traits associated with each sign are listed with the symbol graphs to add to your needlepointing pleasure and to stimulate color and design ideas. Personality traits that are negative, controversial, or suggestive have been deliberately omitted.

These small designs were stitched on 14-mesh canvas with 2-ply

Persian. Aquarius, Gemini, Capricorn, and Cancer were made as a family set, using the same colors in different arrangements. Aries, Leo, and Libra are another group, as are Pisces, Scorpio, and Virgo.

The symbols graphed here can be used individually or in combination with their signs. They are ideal for pictures or coasters (as shown in these photographs). They could also become part of a larger design, such as the "ABC Appliqué Quilt." A symbol might also be added to a "Calendar of Flowers" canvas, a "Special Interests" canvas, or any canvas you wish to make more personal.

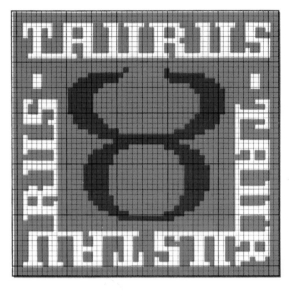

Aries (March 21 –April 19)

The Ram: fire sign, ruled by Mars, the Roman war god; Color: red; Metal: iron; Jewels: aquamarine, bloodstone; Plants: geraniums, honeysuckle; Tree: thorn; Personality: handsome, healthy, independent, restless, impulsive; a pioneer and individualist; a leader

Taurus (April 20 –May 20)

The Bull: earth sign, ruled by Venus, the goddess of love; Color: indigo blue; Metal: copper; Jewel: diamond; Plants: rose, poppy, foxglove; Tree: apple; Personality: appreciative, creative, reliable, good-natured, hard worker; a gourmet and connoisseur of wine; a gardener

Gemini (May 21 –June 20)

The Twins: air sign, ruled by Mercury, the wing-footed messenger god; Color: yellow; Metal: quicksilver; Jewel: emerald; Plants: lily of the valley, lavender; Tree: chestnut; Personality: quick witted, versatile, imaginative, mercurial, brilliant, perpetually youthful; a communicator and intellectual

Cancer or the Moonchild (June 21 –July 22)

The Crab: water sign, ruled by the Moon, goddess of the night and the sea; Colors: violet, ice blue; Metal: silver; Jewel: pearl; Plants: acanthus, anemone; Tree: rubber; Personality: cautious, kind, dependable, faithful, and sensitive; a mother and homebody; a family binder

Leo (July 23–August 22)

The Lion: fire sign, ruled by the Sun, the most powerful god of all; Colors: yellow, orange; Metal: gold; Jewel: ruby; Plants: sunflower, marigold, peony; Tree: palm; Personality: strong, generous, creative, warmhearted, and proud; a king and showman; an executive

Virgo (August 23–September 22)

The Virgin: earth sign, ruled by Mercury, the wing-footed messenger god; Colors: gray, brown; Metal: quicksilver; Jewel: peridot; Plant: morning glory; Tree: hazel; Personality: demure, maidenly, shy, sunny, and dutiful; a perfectionist and health fanatic; a willing worker

Libra (September 23–October 22)

The Balance: air sign, ruled by Venus, the goddess of love; Colors: blue, rose; Metal: copper; Jewel: sapphire; Plants: lilac, vine; Tree: ash; Personality: elegant, poised, curious, sociable, and fashionable: a diplomat and manager; a judge

Scorpio (October 23–November 21)

The Scorpio: water sign, ruled by Mars, the Roman war god, and Pluto, the Roman god of the underworld; Color: red; Metal: iron; Jewel: opal; Plants: carnation, chrysanthemum; Tree: blackthorn; Personality: strong, silent, serious, loyal, and energetic; a spellbinder and a businessperson; a liberated, devoted friend

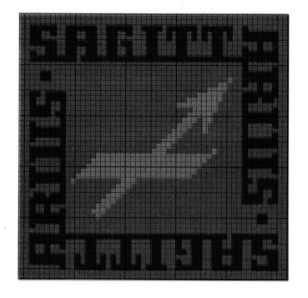

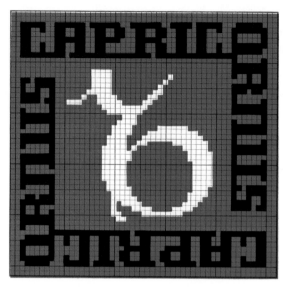

Sagittarius (November 22–December 21)

The Archer: fire sign, ruled by Jupiter, the king of the Roman gods; Color: purple; Metal: tin; Stone: topaz; Plants: mimosa, pinks, dandelions; Trees: lime, oak; Personality: enthusiastic, idealistic, intellectual, confident, . charming; a counselor and a sage; a happy-go-lucky explorer

Capricorn (December 22–January 20)

The Goat: earth sign, ruled by Jupiter, the king of the Roman gods; Colors: blue, black; Metal: lead; Jewels: turquoise, zircon; Plants: pansy, hyacinth, ivy; Tree: pine; Personality: reliable, dependable, respectable, dutiful, and moral; a father figure and a climber; a proper homelover

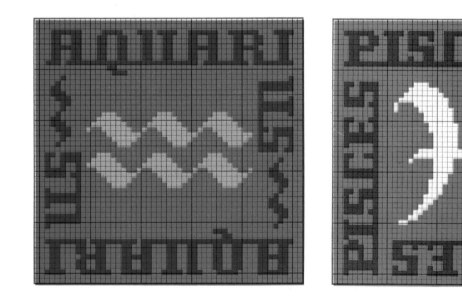

Aquarius (January 21–February 19)

The Water-Bearer: air sign, ruled by Saturn, the father god of Jupiter, and Uranus, the Greek personification of the sky; Color: turquoise; Metal: platinum; Jewel: garnet; Plants: orchid, daffodil; Trees: cherry, peach; Personality: punctual, idealistic, democratic, peaceful, undomesticated; an intellectual

Pisces (February 20–March 20)

The Fishes: water sign, ruled by Neptune, the Roman sea god, and Jupiter, the king of the Roman gods; Color: green; Metal: tin; Jewel: amethyst; Plants: water lily, tulip; Tree: willow; Personality: gentle, hospitable, sensitive, devoted, and dedicated; a philanthropist and dreamer; a lover of animals

CLOCK PILLOW

A clock is a handsome piece of graphic art. Sometimes, it is a reminder of the quick passage of time, but it can also tell us that each moment should be a celebration of life. The hands of this clock can be stopped to record the hour of a happy event. A birth or marriage date and initials might be entered where this stitcher has placed her initials and work date.

The design is composed of elements from a Seth Thomas grandfather clock made in Connecticut in the first half of the nineteenth century. The moon face, a symbol of the lunar calendar, usually revolved in these old clocks to show the different phases of the moon or the seasons. The dials could be set to chime on the quarter hours and to strike on the hour. The original clock was tall, with the moon and the two dials in one box at the top and the clock face decorated with painted roses in a box under it. For this design, all the motifs were incorporated within the single clockface.

This design would also be effective as a picture, or as a cover for a stool, a chair, or an album.

Clock Pillow

Canvas: 14-mesh mono

Yarn: Persian (2 ply)

Stitches: Tent; light gold background, Continuous Mosaic; outer border, Slanted Gobelin (over two canvas threads)

Finishing: 13½ by 14 inches, backed with brown velvet (2 inches at sides for boxing)

FOR OUR CHILDREN

The objects in this section are not only for our children but also for our children's children. A piece of needlework made with high hopes and magnificent skill and dedicated to a young person is a very flattering and thrilling gift, particularly if the piece has taken shape before the child's very eyes. Surely, it will always hang in a special place in his or her own home. And how enjoyable it will be for the young person to tell his or her children why and how and when it was made. A perfect example is the "Horn of Plenty Picture."

An appliqué quilt made for a grandchild will surely belong to his or her child one day, and the grandmother who made it will then be a great grandmother and will remember the pleasure of making it to celebrate the arrival of that grandchild. The "Twelve Days of Christmas Sock" will no doubt become a family tradition, and the stitcher and her family will love it more with every Christmas. The "American Primitive Sampler" will be enjoyed by the parents of the stitcher with much pride, and her children and grandchildren will learn that she loved needlework so much that she stitched a celebration of her childhood for them to enjoy. Any little child loves to see his name spelled out, but in the "Provincial Birth Record," he will also see representations of his mother and father and himself as a baby. Certainly, this picture will be carefully preserved to be hung in future nurseries.

AMERICAN PRIMITIVE SAMPLER

(SEE PAGE 118)

American folk art has come of age. A major exhibition at the Whitney Museum of Art in 1974, entitled "Flowering of American Folk Art (1776-1876)," firmly established this fact. It is not only appreciated by collectors of Americana and by American art historians but is now generally recognized by the rest of the world as a great heritage.

Folk art, which has its roots in crafts, was the work of simple, unpretentious, untrained rural artists. The results are primitive, naïve, and completely fascinating. In addition to paintings, many outstanding examples have survived in the form of objects that were designed or ornamented for daily use: quilts and other bed coverings, needlepoint and other embroidery, rugs, carved objects, furniture, tableware, and shop signs. The strong American folk art influence reflected in this sampler and throughout this book is offered in happy recognition of these American artists as a tribute to their uninhibited creativity.

In the first hundred years of America's independence, it was a practical necessity for a young girl to be taught sewing at home at an early age. In school, painting and embroidery were her major subjects. She made a sampler to display her knowledge of stitchery. It was hung with pride first in her parents' home and then in her own home. Eventually, it became a family heirloom. These samplers often included alphabets, architectural scenes, and biographical information.

This "American Primitive Sampler" shows the interior of a house occupied by a mother, father, and four children. There is space at the bottom for the family history or a simple biography of the stitcher. The garden border and all the furnishings, people, and clothing were inspired by items from the great Whitney Museum show.

The sampler can be altered to represent the stitcher's family by simply changing the color of hair and eyes and the number of children. The age of the stitcher need not be noted, but I believe that one's age is important for its historical significance as a part of a family record.

This sampler is made up of relatively few stitches, but they are utilized to their fullest by turning them in various directions. This is a splendid way to display your needlepoint skill and at the same time create an heirloom with your personal biography for your family to enjoy.

Various yarns, as well as various stitches, should be used in a sampler. Wool twist is excellent for the Petit Point and petit stitches because its smooth 4-ply texture fits this 14-to-the-inch stitchery perfectly. The full 3-ply Persian wool fits the Rep background exceptionally well.

Although this sampler was made as a soft hanging, it may also be stretched and framed. Various parts of the design could be used individually. A little picture could be made from the child's room; a cushion, from the living room; a large pillow or a chair seat, from the two side panel designs of robins in trees framing a message or a monogram. The small repeat pattern on the wall of the children's bedroom would be charming for the seat of a little child's chair.

PROVINCIAL BIRTH RECORD

(SEE PAGE 124)

This provincial family has its roots in eighteenth- and nineteenth-century folk art from the Alsatian region of Europe. Simple peasant figures of this type were used to decorate home furnishings and toys, and the tradition was brought to America by German, Swiss, and French immigrants.

This birth record, which was stitched by a loving aunt, documents the young person's name and birth date and the full names of his parents. It is a permanent record worthy of becoming a family legacy.

The little border of geometric white flowers might be used for a belt or for luggage rack straps or as a border for another design. The family group, either by itself or framed by the floral border, might be used to make a small pillow. The basic geometric arrangement of the design might be used for a family record with another design from these pages inserted in the square opening.

HORN OF PLENTY PICTURE

(SEE PAGE 126)

A cornucopia, or goat's horn, that overflows with fruit and ears of grain was first used as a decorative motif signifying abundance by the ancient Greeks. In Greek mythology, the goat's horn was considered both male and female in form and thus became symbolic of prosperity. What a happy symbol of riches to stitch for someone for whom you wish the best in life!

This horn of plenty, with its richly colored design and natural background, was framed as a picture with a stitched white mat border, but it would also make a lovely tray or tabletop.

TWELVE DAYS OF CHRISTMAS SOCK

(SEE PAGE 128)

Here is a Christmas sock big enough to hold goodies for a flock of children and lovely enough to appeal to the whole family. An infant can enjoy the little animals and people; a kindergartener, the sequence of numbers; an older child, the pictorial representation of the charming old carol, with its persistent refrain. For adults, there is the symbolism of the carol. In Christian symbolism, the partridge, famous for deserting its young, indicates abandonment of faith; so perhaps the true love in the carol gives the partridge ensconced in a pear tree as a token that he will not leave. Or perhaps the gifts are penances for a failure to observe the rituals of the twelve days of Christmas (the time between Christmas and Epiphany).

The individual designs would make charming Christmas tree ornaments if stitched on small pieces of canvas. They might be used for pincushions, eyeglass cases, or small Easter and Valentine's Day gifts or to decorate purses or tote bags. They could also be worked in Gros Point or Petit Point, with or without the numbers to make pictures for a child's room.

ABC APPLIQUÉ QUILT

(SEE PAGE 130)

Quilt making in America took two forms. One was the *patchwork quilt* which was made of hundreds of pieces of fabric sewn together in a pattern and then quilted. The second form, the *appliqué quilt,* was often more skillfully executed. It was composed of individual motifs, such as hearts and flowers, cut from fabrics of various patterns, sewn onto a background fabric, and then quilted.

If this ABC design had been made into a real quilt, it would have been called a *story quilt* because it is made to entertain. Because of its relatively small size, it would have been considered a *cradle quilt.* Because it is carefully divided into individual geometric units, it would have been labeled an *album quilt.* A story-cradle-album-appliqué-quilt needlepoint picture.

But no matter what its label, it is a charming picture for a child's room and a grandmother's delight to make. Because there are twenty-six letters in the alphabet but thirty boxes in this design, the four remaining boxes were used for the child's name, birth date, and zodiac sign and hour of birth and the grandmother's name and the year the picture was stitched.

Any of these little designs and letters could be used individually or in groups for smaller gifts of needlepoint. The entire piece could be enlarged, using a 5- or 4-to-the-inch canvas and heavy rug wool, to make a cheerful rug.

American Primitive Sampler

Canvas: 7/14-mesh Penelope

Yarn: wool twist, light yellow and rust Persian, silk for faces and white accents on clothing

Stitches: Areas not specifically listed on the following pages are worked in Petit Point.

Backstitch is added to fill in spaces between rows where needed. Don't be afraid to improvise.

Finished size: 26½ by 33¼ inches

Living Room

Stitches: father's coat, boy's coat, picture frame, Continuous Mosaic; father's vest, vertical Kalem one-way right (fourteen stitches to 1 inch both ways); mother's dress, Kalem horizontal and vertical (fourteen stitches to 1 inch both ways); curtains, mother's bonnet, boy's collar, girl's apron, Mosaic; girl's skirt and pantaloons, boy's trousers, stool cover, stripes in wallpaper, Rep; between wallpaper stripes, Backstitch; rug, horizontal Kalem (seven stitches to 1 horizontal inch, fourteen stitches to 1 vertical inch); fireplace frame, Slanted Gobelin, Flat, Kalem one-way right (seven stitches to 1 horizontal inch, fourteen stitches to 1 vertical inch); hearth, Flat Chequer; bricks, Cashmere; flames, Florentine or Flame

Children's Room

Stitches: stenciled wallpaper flowers, four Mosaics to center; stenciled wallpaper stripes, Rep; quilt, Flat, Mosaic; picture frame, Slanted Gobelin; blue and gold valance, Mosaic, Rep

Entrance and Kitchen

Stitches: clock inner panel, tabletop, Continuous Mosaic; clock outline, blue doorframe, Mosaic; rust doorframe, Rep; blue door panels, Cross; doorknob, Asterisk; floor, Cushion Chequer; compote, Slanted Gobelin

Blue outer frame

Stitches: Kalem, seven stitches to 1 horizontal or vertical inch; Backstitch, seven stitches to 1 inch; Flat, padded corners, fourteen stitches to 1 inch both ways

Side and top panels

Stitches: yellow background, tree trunks, leaves, Rep; vases, Mosaic Chequer; flowers, Mosaic; sun, Mosaic and Crossed Mosaic; chimney, Cashmere; nest, Kalem one-way left (seven stitches to 1 horizontal inch, fourteen stitches to 1 vertical inch), Gros Point; robins, Kalem one-way right (seven stitches to 1 horizontal inch, fourteen stitches to 1 vertical inch), Continuous Mosaic

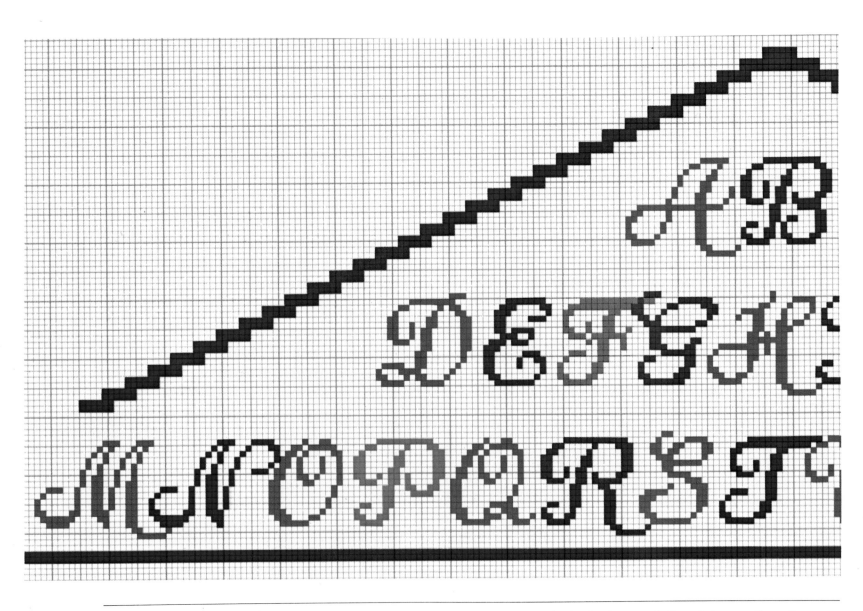

House frame and lettering

Stitches: roof, Rep (fourteen stitches to 1 horizontal inch, seven stitches to 1 vertical inch); background, Gros Point; outlines, Rep; rust outlines, Rep; red dividers, stem with yellow Backstitch

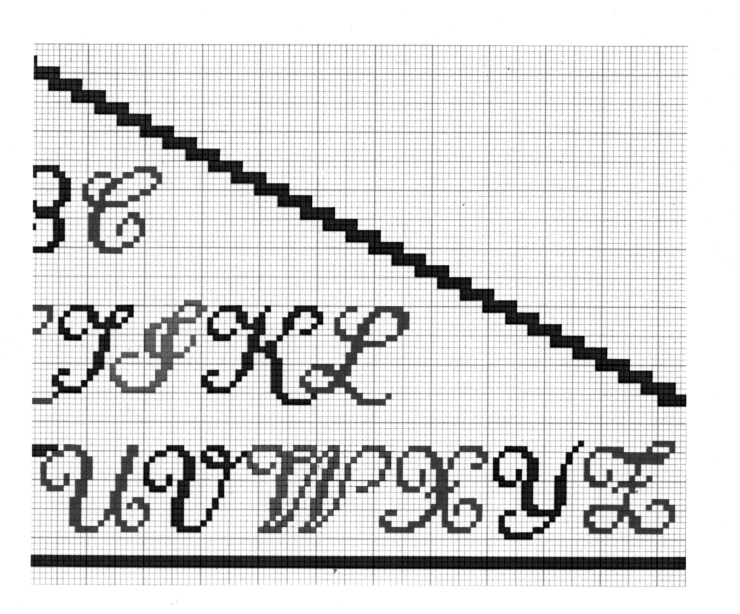

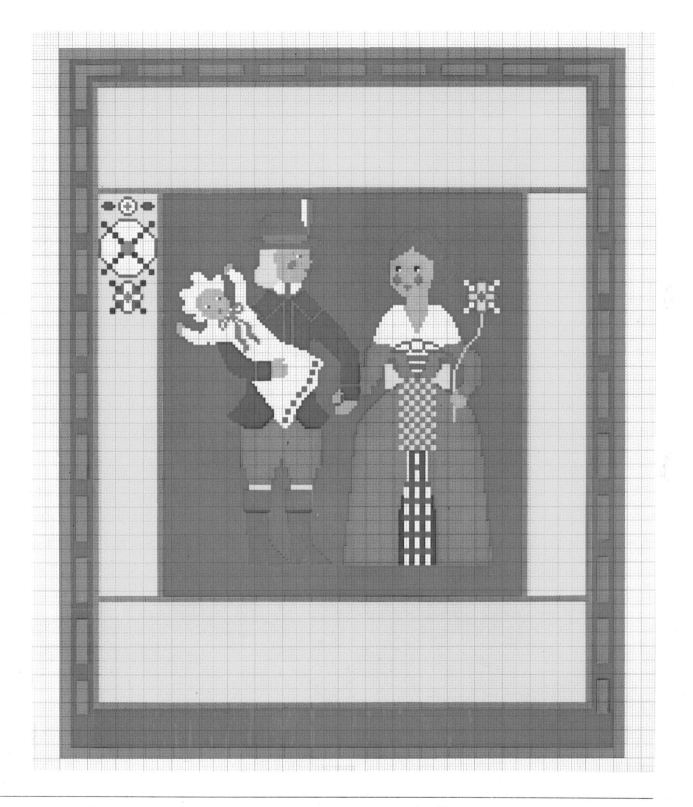

Provincial Birth Record

Canvas: 14-mesh mono

Yarn: Persian (2 ply)

Stitches: picture, Tent, vertical and horizontal Slanted Gobelin (two directions), Mosaic (two directions); picture background, Mosaic Chequer; lettering, Tent with Slanted Gobelin accents; lettering background, Continuous Mosaic; side panels, Tent, Mosaic (two directions), Cross; blue border, Mosaic, with pink Flat insertions; pink outlines, Slanted Gobelin (two directions); inscription and background in blue border, Tent

Finished size: 19¼ by 14¾ inches

HORN of PLENTY — Symbol of Abundance

for my daughter Linda in the year 1975
by Patti Baker Russell

**Horn of Plenty
Picture**

Canvas: 18-mesh mono

Yarn: Persian (1 ply)

Stitches: design, lettering, and border, Tent; accents on lettering, Slanted Gobelin; background, Continuous Mosaic

Finished size (and framed): 13½ by 13 inches, mounted on a stretcher

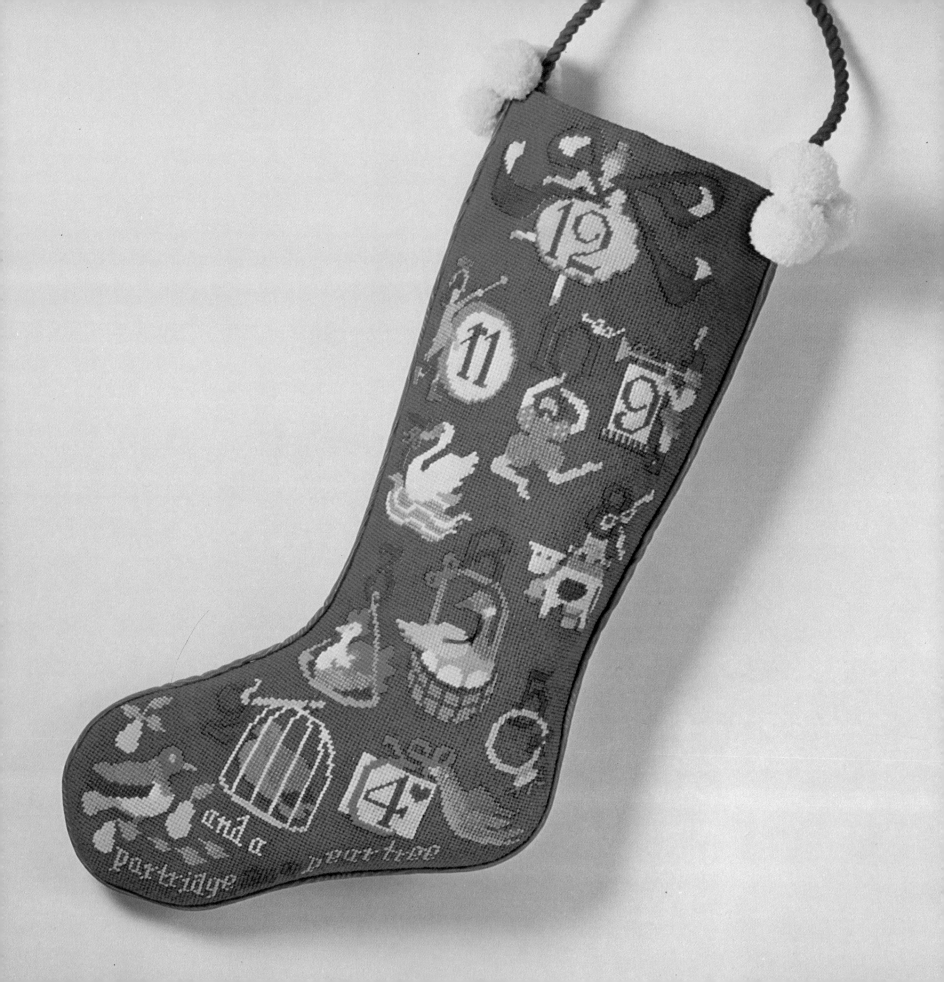

*Twelve Days of
Christmas Sock*

Canvas: 12-mesh mono

Yarn: Persian (2 ply), wool twist

Stitches: Tent

Finished size: 23¾ by 10¼ inches, measured
top to toe

ABC Appliqué Quilt

Canvas: 10-mesh mono

Yarn: Persian

Stitches: pictures and background, Tent; lettering, slanted Gobelin; light blue borders, dark blue border and accents, Cushion

Finishing: 27 by 31 inches, mounted on a stretcher

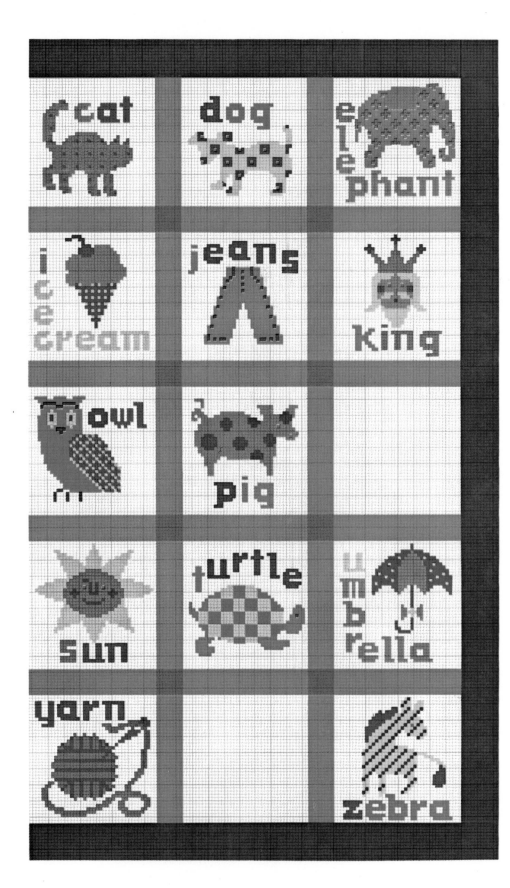

SPECIAL INTERESTS

What are the special interests of the members of your family? Does your home reflect these interests? Here is a group of decorative objects designed for you to needlepoint as tributes to their hobbies, occupations, and activities. It includes designs celebrating Americana collections and collectors, shops and shop owners, medicine and doctors, painting and painters, gardening and gardeners, writing and readers, needlework and needleworkers, music and musicians, food and cooks.

Other interests can be reflected by adapting designs from other sections of this book to fit these objects. For example, law can be represented by the scales of the Libra zodiac sign; sports, by the athletic figures of the Gemini sign; fishing, from the fish of the Pisces sign; flowers, from the "Calendar of Flowers."

By adding appropriate messages or inscriptions, you will create highly personal pieces of needlework that reflect individuality and warmth.

OPEN AND CLOSED SIGN

(SEE PAGE 142)

Because morning glories are gloriously wide open in the morning and fold like little old umbrellas later in the day, they illustrate the message of this sign. Although this piece is designed for an office or a shop, it might be amusing to use at home. Many people close their kitchens, bars, or bedrooms at certain hours, and this pretty needlepoint sign is a nice way to convey the message. The lettering could also read "Awake" and "Asleep," "Come In" and "Go Away," or "In" and "Out." The two pieces of needlepoint were mounted separately and then placed back to back and put in a single frame so that the sign can be turned to the appropriate message.

The wreaths of open and closed morning glories would make a

charming pair of pillows. They could also adorn the front and back of a tote bag or purse, with a monogram or first name placed in the center.

AMERICAN EAGLE PILLOW

(SEE PAGE 146)

If your special interest is Americana, here is a dyed-in-the-wool American eagle. The bald or white-headed eagle, noted for its size, strength, and powers of flight and vision, was used extensively in the arts after the inauguration of George Washington. It was adopted by Congress in 1782 for the Great Seal of the United States and became our national emblem. The eagle is derived from the patterns used in jacquard coverlets. In the 1820s, the jacquard loom, the invention of a French weaver named Joseph Jacquard, was introduced to America. The flying shuttle for this new hand-operated loom made it possible to weave large unseamed coverlets with complicated patterns. The use of hand-spun and home-dyed wool preserved the handcrafted quality in these early jacquards. Many patterns were used, but rosettes, urns, and eagles were the favorites.

Popular color combinations included shades of indigo blue on blue; blue and white; red and white; red, white, and indigo; and red, gold, blue, and white. Other hand-dyed colors included rust, brown, tan, and light and dark green. By using these ranges of color, you will give this pillow (or any other appropriate piece of needlework) an authentic early American quality.

This American eagle design could be adapted very effectively to make chair pads for an early American straight-backed chair or for a rocking chair.

SHOP SIGN

(SEE PAGE 148)

Historically, a trade or shop sign reflected the taste and status of the merchant or craftsman who displayed it. Throughout the nineteenth century, people used painted shop signs in the form of either carved figures that stood on the sidewalk in front of a shop or panels that hung over the entrance. Panel shop signs were especially popular for taverns and were often painted in exchange for food and a night's lodging. The first commercial artists painted these signs for the edification of the large illiterate population.

Because of its simplicity, the classic shield shape of this sign is well suited to mounting over wood. The finials are wood turnings painted gold and attached after the needlepoint has been mounted. This piece was done by the owners of a frame shop and art gallery, but it would also be appropriate for a kitchen, family room, or study, reflecting a special interest, hobby, or profession. The mortar-and-pestle design could be used for any profession relating to medicine. The open book suggests not only literary people but teachers and church people. The lyre is for any musical hobby.

In addition to the designs shown here, there are many other designs in the book that would fit in this basic sign. The clock would suggest antiques or a special interest in timepieces. The various designs for the "Calendar of Flowers" would be appropriate for gardeners or plant lovers; the eagle, for a collector of American antiques; the horn of plenty, for a gourmet cook, a gardener, or a farmer. And for a highly individual celebration of a special person, many motifs might be combined and perhaps scaled down to make a "This Is Your Life" assemblage.

NEEDLEWORK BOX

(SEE PAGE 154)

At one time, a needlewoman kept her sewing gear in a carefully fitted little case called an *etui*. It was made of silver or gilt or padded satin decorated with embroidery, and it dangled from the waist of her voluminous skirt. Besides a thimble, scissors, and needles, she might also have carefully fitted into the case other objects of everyday use, such as a knife and fork that screwed into separate silver handles, a toothpick, an ear-spoon, a buttonhook, a pen, a rule, and a pair of compasses. In the seventeenth and eighteenth centuries, she wore a chatelaine or *nécessaire*. It, too, hung from the waist, but each item was on an individual chain: scissors in a case, a thimble in a thimble barrel, needles in a needlecase, a pincushion, and perhaps a graphite pencil, a writing tablet, and a scent bottle.

But skirts became narrower, big pockets disappeared, and elegant workboxes sat on tables. Today, these old boxes are collector's items. They were the combined efforts of various skilled craftsmen who outfitted them with tools. They often held dressing table items, as well as writing equipment and sewing gear.

This beautiful workbox was once a humble wooden cigar box; now, it is covered with needlepoint and lined with moiré. It can sit on a table beside a needlepointer, holding her scissors, thimble, needles, tape measure, sewing glasses, pencil, and emery board.

The cigar box is 9¼ inches long, 1½ inches high, and 6⅜ inches deep. A new cover was cut to fit over the top of the box, because its original cover was recessed; it is 9¼ inches by 6⅜ inches, the same size as the box itself. The original hinges were saved and reused.

The finished needlepoint is 9⅞ inches by 7⅛ inches, allowing ⅝ inch for the flaps on all four sides of the cover. At the four corners of the top, diagonal lines were drawn on the canvas five stitches away from the actual corners, and these areas were left unstitched. This, in effect, created slanted corners so that the needlepoint could be neatly eased when mounted.

A single strip of needlepoint, 32 by 1½ inches, was made to wrap around the four sides of the box itself.

The scissors that decorate the lid of this workbox were copied from antique Chinese snipping scissors. The fretwork, although it is called a *Greek key,* is an authentic Chinese pattern. The scissors were stitched in Tent and then overstitched in places with Slanted Gobelin; the screw is Asterisk. The Slanted Gobelin stitches in the Greek key border change direction at the center of each side of the cover. The Florentine starts at center front and is worked in slanted rows to the corners of the Greek key motif (at the corners of the box) and changes direction.

Another motif symbolizing a different hobby might be substituted for the scissors and thimble.

BON APPÉTIT
CHAIR CUSHIONS OR PLAQUES

(SEE PAGE 156)

Needlepoint often appeals to creative people who love gourmet cooking. This needlepoint project combines the two skills. A set of *bon appétit* chair seats will delight your guests' eyes before your cooking delights their palates.

The animal figurines, decorated with vines and berries, were inspired by Delft ceramic pieces from the eighteenth century, which, in turn, were inspired by Far Eastern art. This Dutch chinaware is famous for its blue-and-white or polychrome decorations. The pieces of decorative faience, which included tiles, plaques, and figurines, had dark or white backgrounds.

There are eight animal motifs: cow, hen, pig, goose, rabbit, goat, lamb, and fish. The cow and the hen are resting in beds of red and yellow flowers. The other patterns shown as tiles or plaques were designed to fit into the same flowered motif for use as chair seats, cushions, or pillows. As plaques, they serve two purposes: They can hang on a wall as decorations, and they can be placed on the dining table as mats for hot serving dishes. If you use rings to hang them, they will lie flat when they are put on the table.

Individually or separately, these designs would make charming nursery pictures; the fish and the goose might enliven the front and the back of a summer tote bag. The eight motifs, each with its own bed of flowers, would make a delightful rug.

THE NATURALIST TAPESTRY

(SEE PAGE 168)

This is a picture of natural things—a bird, a bee, a butterfly, fruit, flowers, a shell, and a coral branch—all drawn in the fantasy manner of Louis XVI embellishment. Louis's wife, Marie Antoinette, of "let them eat cake" fame, fancied herself a country girl. At the opulent palace of Versailles, she had a doll's house hamlet built. There, dressed in pretty peasant dresses, she imagined herself leading a real country life. Only a few intimates were permitted to visit her there.

Far from being a social commentary, however, this representation of the pretty side of nature celebrates its beauty and is appropriate for a contemporary home. A tall fire screen on a stand would be a lovely way to display this, or it could be made into a low, square screen to hide the black bareness of a hearth or an air-conditioning unit (when not in use). It would also make an elegant chair back or cover for a dressing table bench.

Every needlepointer, at one time or another, should work on a frame. In only a short time, you can acquire the knack of the two-hand method of stitching, poking in from the top with one hand and up from underneath with the other. The position of your body in relation to the frame is the most important factor. Sit up straight, on your "sitting bone," and never bend over your work. Backache can be prevented only if you give careful consideration to posture, chair height, and the distance of the frame from your body. Sit at the frame, create your beautiful tapestry, and muse on the country life.

Open and
Closed Sign

Canvas: 14-mesh mono

Yarn: Persian (2 ply)

Stitches: lettering, Mosaic with Slanted Gobelin and Tent outlines; design and background, Tent

Finished size: 8 by 14 inches, mounted on a stretcher

American Eagle Pillow

Canvas: 12-mesh mono

Yarn: Persian (2 ply except where noted)

Stitches: top of shield, Continuous Mosaic; shield stripes, Slanted Gobelin; octagonal border, Straight Gobelin (3 ply); background outside border, Hungarian lettering, Slanted Gobelin and Tent; design and background within border, Tent

Finished size: 16 by 17 inches

Shop Sign

Canvas: 14-mesh mono

Yarn: Persian (2 ply)

Stitches: largest lettering, Mosaic with Slanted Gobelin and Tent outlines; medium-sized lettering, Slanted Gobelin with Tent outlines; small lettering, Slanted Gobelin for capitals, Tent for lowercase; dabs of paint, Continuous Mosaic; palette and brushes, Tent; brown background, Continuous Mosaic, with Tent behind lettering

Finished size: 24 by 15 by ⅝ inches

149

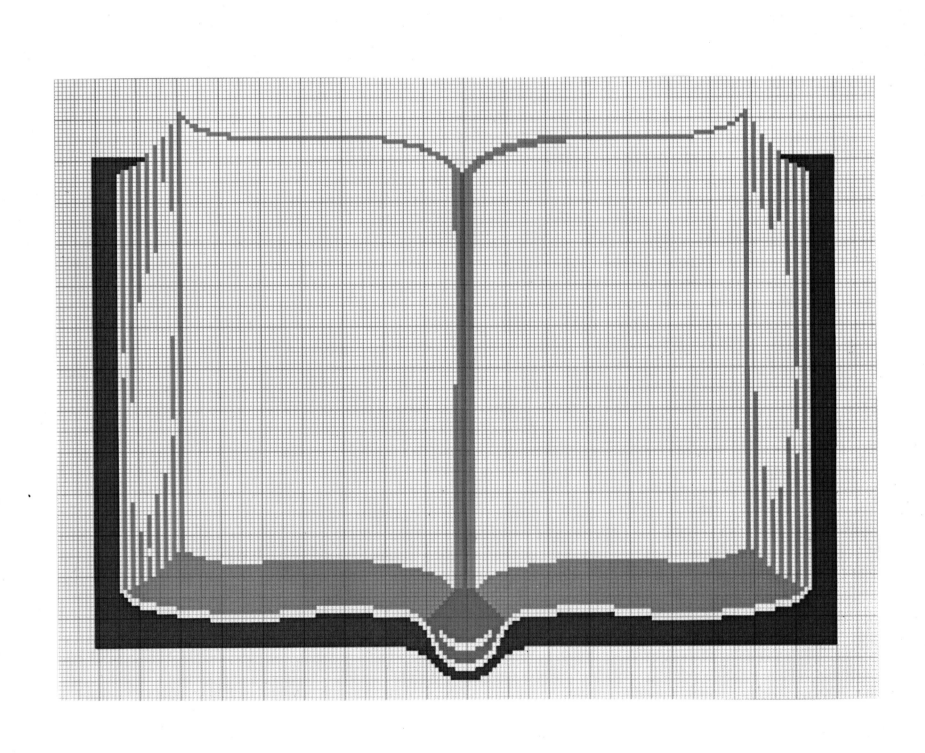

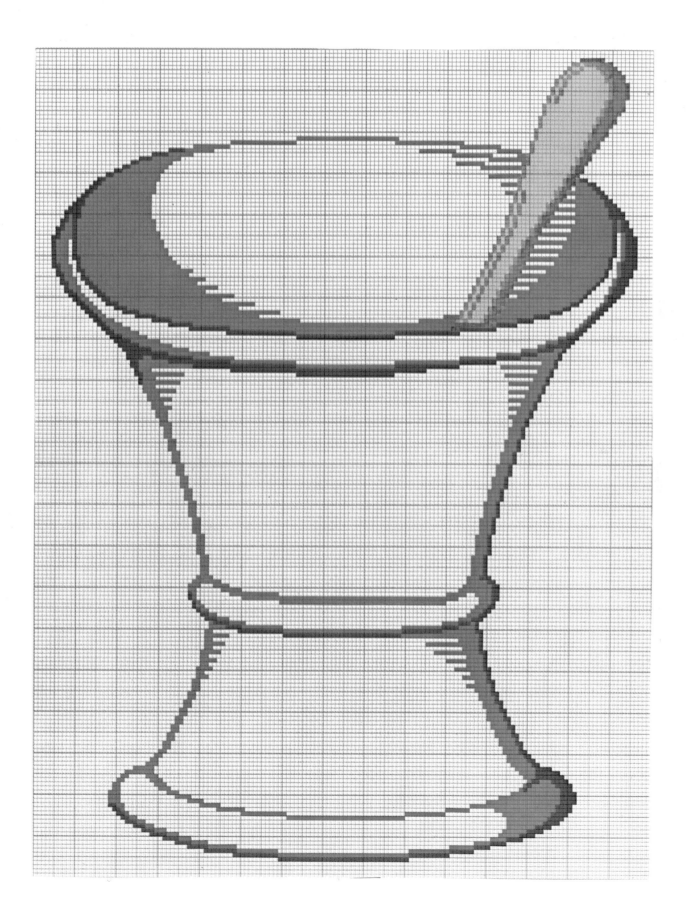

151

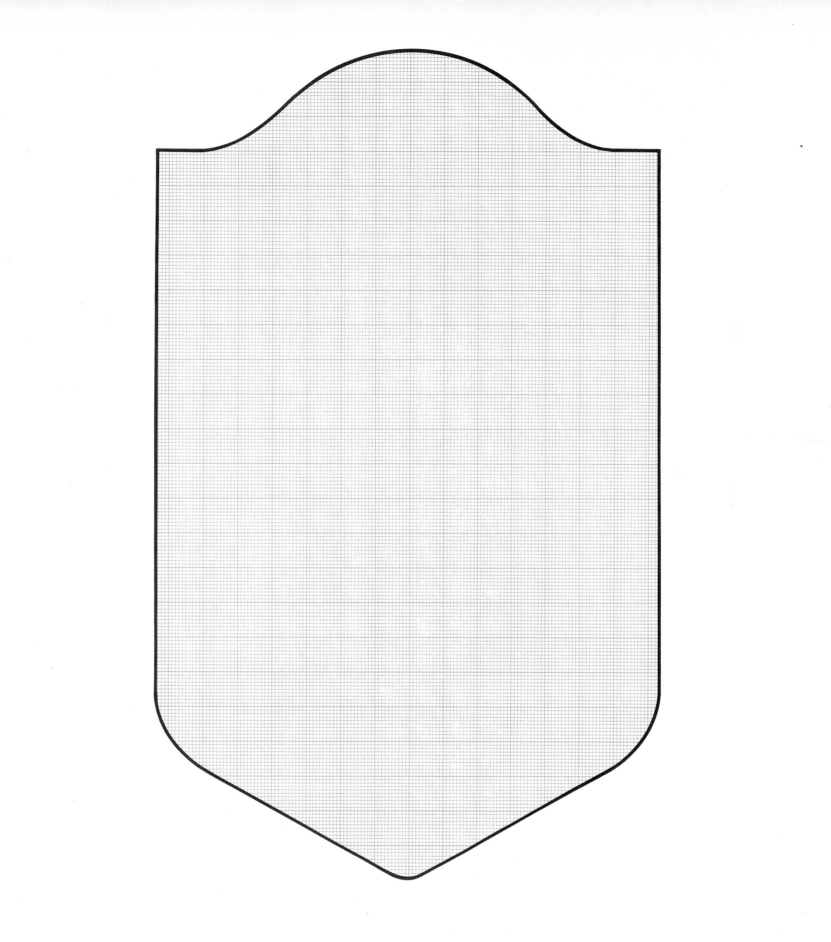

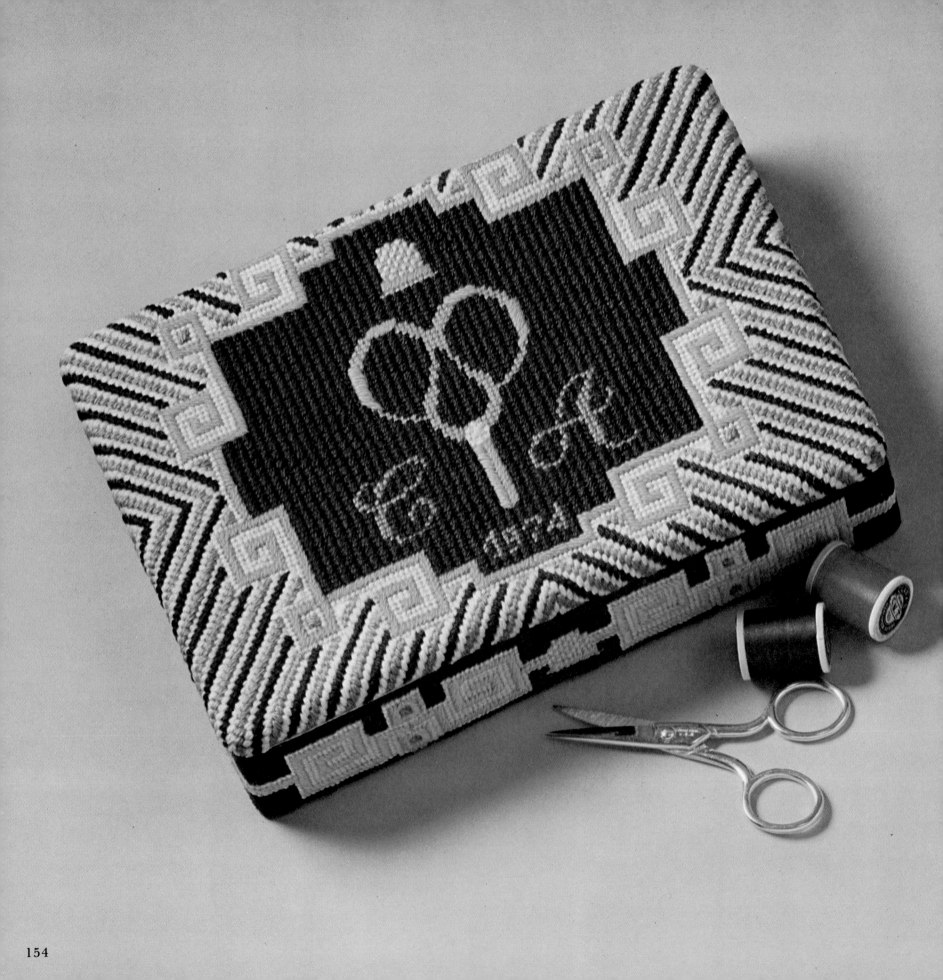

Needlework Box

Canvas: 14-mesh mono

Yarn: Persian (2 ply except where noted)

Stitches: navy background, vertical rib Rep; scissors, Tent and Slanted Gobelin with Asterisk; thimble, Tent and Slanted Gobelin; initials and date, Tent; Greek key border, Slanted Gobelin; white border background, Tent; blue and white diagonal stripes, Florentine; navy diagonal background for sides of box, Tent

Finished size: 6¾ by 9½ by 2 inches

155

Bon Appétit Cushions

Canvas: 12-mesh mono

Yarn: Persian (2 ply)

Stitches: Tent

Finishing: 14 by 16 inches, mounted as chair cushions; 1½ inches of fabric boxing

Bon Appétit Plaques

Canvas: 12-mesh mono

Yarn: Persian (2 ply), light blue wool twist

Stitches: Tent; checked bands, Flat

Finished size: 10½ by 10½ inches

160

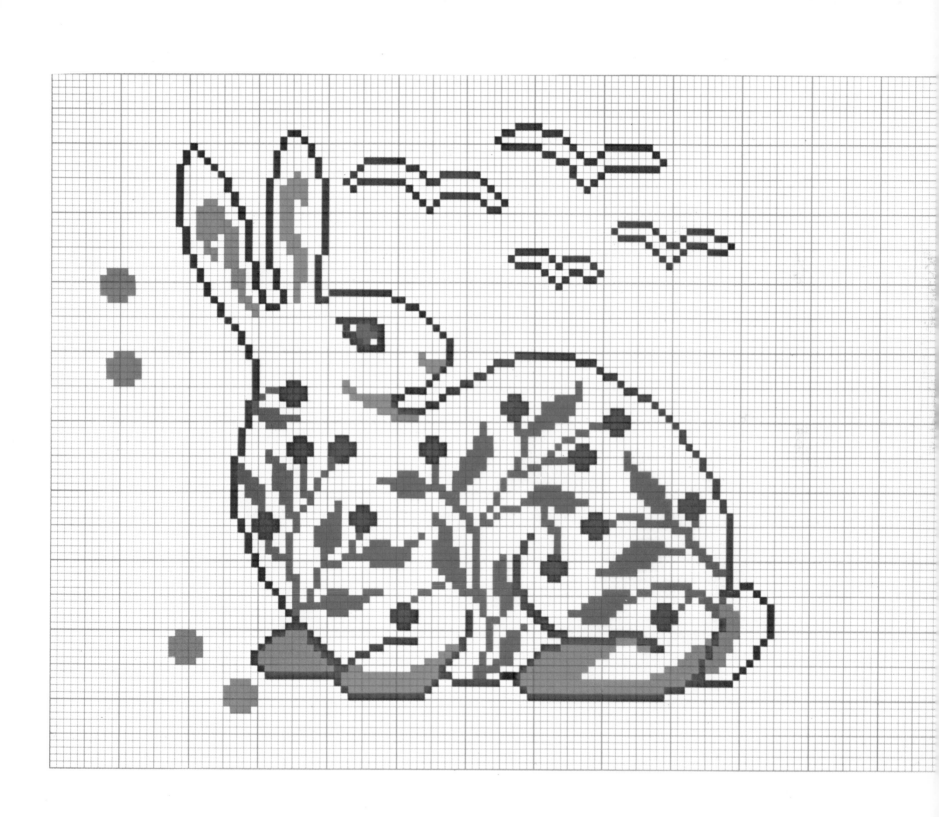

162

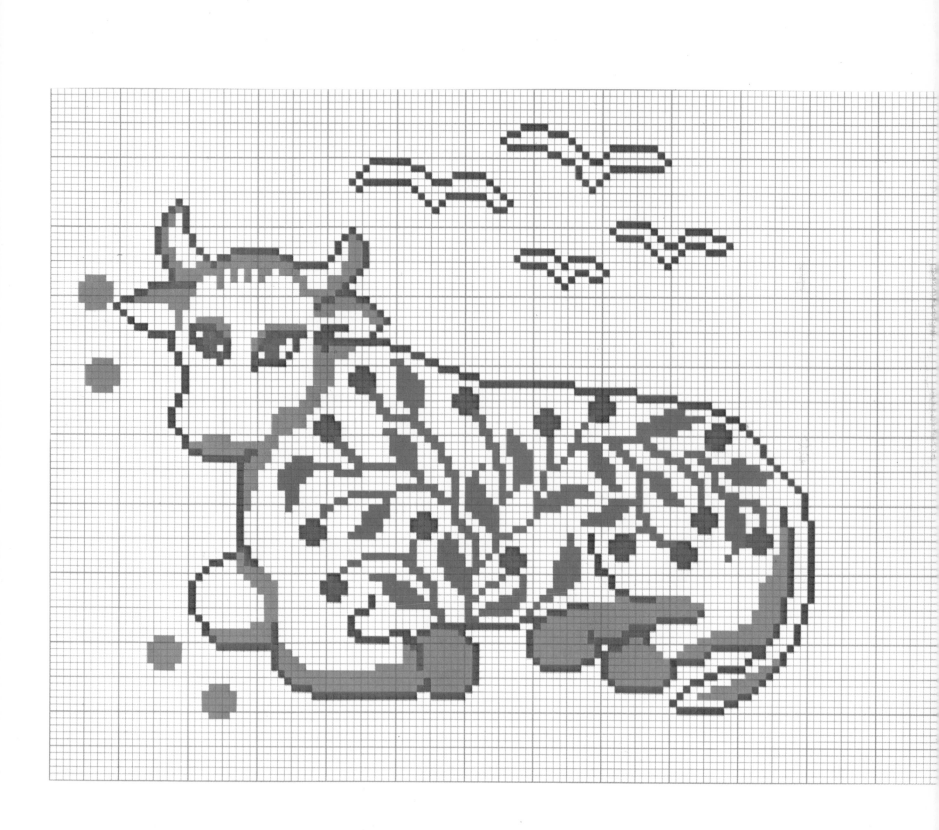

164

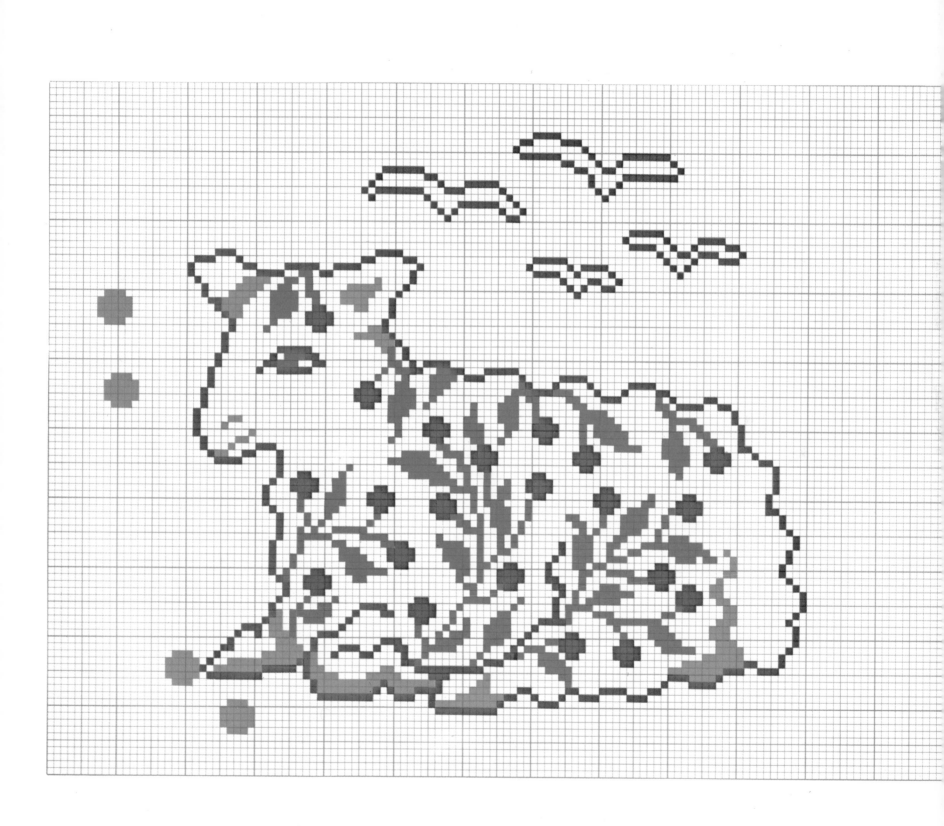

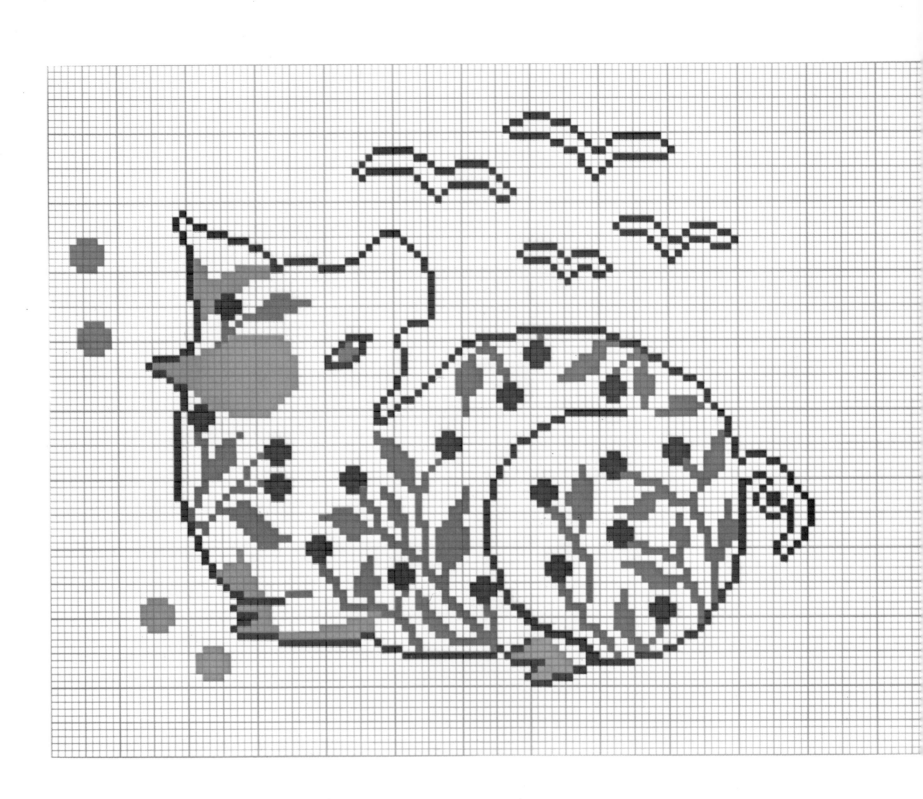

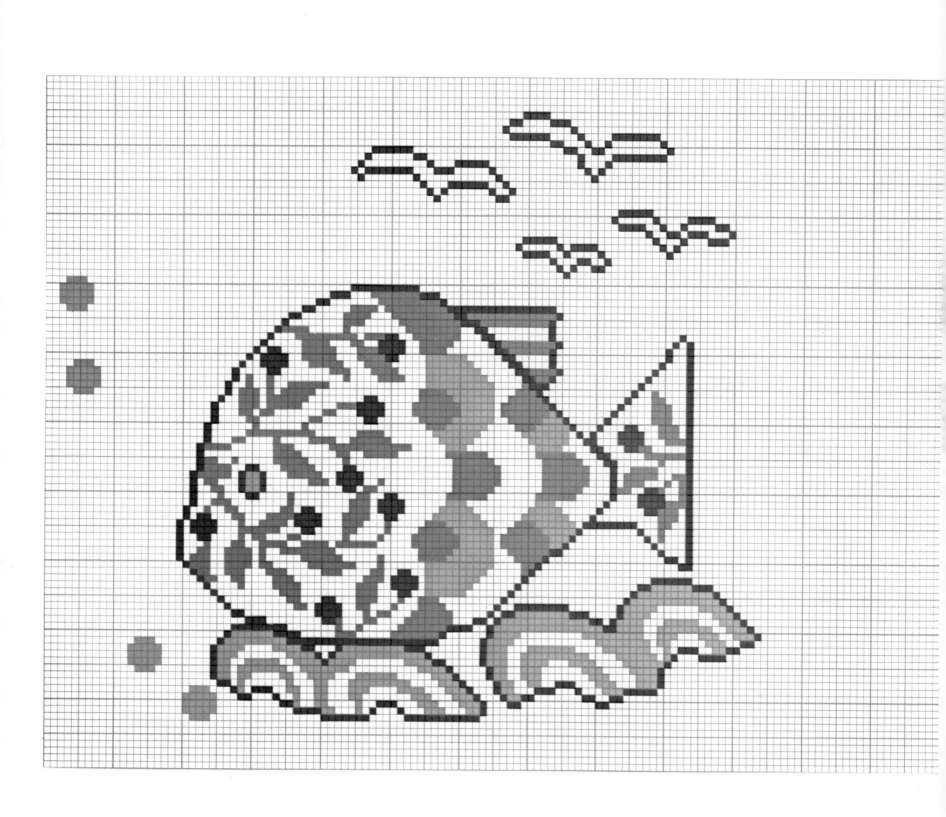

The Naturalist Tapestry

Canvas: 14-mesh mono

Yarn: Persian

Stitches: design and background, Tent (2 ply);
border, vertical Rep in diagonal rows

Finished size: 23½ by 21½ inches

169

MATERIALS AND HOW TO START AND FINISH

CANVAS

Canvas is the even, open-weave mesh to be covered by the needlepoint stitches. There are two kinds of canvas: mono and Penelope. **Mono** canvas is a basketweave mesh formed by single horizontal filling threads weaving in and out of single vertical warp threads. **Penelope** canvas has two closely woven horizontal filling threads that weave in and out of two closely woven vertical warp threads. This crossing of two threads by two threads creates even squares of four canvas threads.

    Size numbers refer to the number of vertical canvas threads to the inch across the width of the canvas.

    Mono canvas is described by a single number because of the single-thread weave. The Mono canvases used in this book are generally 10, 12, and 14 mesh. The "Horn of Plenty Picture" uses an 18-mesh canvas. Mono canvas also comes in 16 and 24 mesh.

    Penelope canvas is described by two numbers separated by a slash mark. The first number indicates the number of double or Gros Point threads to the inch; the second number refers to the number of single or Petit Point threads. The "Endless Knot Wedding Picture" is worked on a 10/20 Penelope canvas; the "American Primitive Sampler" is worked on a 7/14 Penelope canvas. When using a variety of stitches, I prefer to work on a Penelope canvas because the stitch sizes can be varied easily by using it for both regular size and petit stitches.

    Canvas quality varies. Some canvas is woven of tightly spun smooth threads that retain their body and resist distortion. The number of threads to the inch from selvage to selvage may be quite even, but there can be fewer stitches to the inch in the other direction. This creates a problem for anyone working a graphed or counted-thread design. If the canvas is held with the selvage at one side, the piece will be higher than it is wide for the same number of stitches. This is quite undesirable when making a square pillow, but you can compensate for the discrepancy either by adding rows of stitches to the top and bottom or by turning the canvas so that the selvage is at the lower edge. If you are making a set of anything, be sure that you are consistent in the placement of the selvages; otherwise, the piece will not match.

Other canvas may have a very even thread count in both directions. For this reason, the "Calendar of Flowers" designs, which have counted-thread, graphed borders, were put on an even-thread canvas. However, it tends to distort and may become limp quickly. If you are working on such a canvas, remember to keep a loose stitch tension and handle the canvas with care.

YARN

Persian is now a generic term referring to a 3-ply long-haired needlepoint wool. The Paternayan Brothers of New York City were the first spinners and dyers of Persian wool. Originally, they imported it for the repair of Persian carpets. Now, because it is particularly suitable for canvas embroidery, they distribute it for needlepoint throughout the United States. Most of the projects in *Needlepoint Celebrations* use Persian wool. And you need not hesitate to substitute it in those cases where some other yarn has been used.

When Persian is used for Tent on 10-mesh canvas, it is used as it comes (the full 3-plies). On 12- and 14-mesh canvas, it should be split and used 2 ply. On 18-mesh canvas, a single ply is used.

Nantucket, a wool twist, is the only other wool used for the designs in this book. It is smoother than Persian but can be used with the same canvas without obtaining a remarkable difference in texture. It is more costly than Persian, but it is available in a clearer color palette, which is sometimes of great value. Wool twist is a fine 4-ply yarn. All 4 plies should be used on 12- or 14-mesh canvas, but it can be split for very fine work. (Note: If Nantucket is not available at your needlepoint supply shop, you can write to Nantucket Needleworks, Nantucket Island, Massachusetts 02554.)

French silk may be inconvenient to locate and costly to purchase, but the color and texture are so lovely that you might try it for one precious picture. It is a 7-ply yarn and is used as it comes on 12- or 14-mesh canvas, but it should be split for work on finer mesh. (Note: You can write to either of these sources to locate French silk: Handwork Tapestries, 240 Lambert Avenue, Copaigue, New York 11726, or Scandinavian Art Handicraft, 7696 Camargo Road, Cincinnati, Ohio 45243.)

A word of caution: Be very careful about wetting silk. A silk piece should be only lightly misted with water on the back when blocked; otherwise, it may run. Silk dulls from much handling. In working the "American Primitive Sampler," I tacked small pieces of cheesecloth over the silk areas as I finished them. A soft, clean linen towel was kept over the worked areas that were rolled and pinned out of the way.

D. M. C. cotton may be substituted for silk. Use the strands as they come, and double them through the eye of the needle to equal 7-ply silk.

Note: Use the full strands of yarn (i.e., all the plies) for the designs in this book unless the instructions specifically call for the yarn to be split.

NEEDLES

The best needles available are English steel needles. Size 18 is suitable for 10- or 12-mesh; size 20, for 14-mesh canvas; and size 22, for 18-mesh canvas. The needle should be fairly easy to thread, but the yarn must not keep slipping out of the eye. I prefer a needle that is too small to one that is too large because when the eye is excessively large, it is difficult to draw the bulky needle and the yarn that is doubled over it through the canvas.

Threading the needle with wool requires a special technique. The spit-and-poke method is not for wool. Instead, wrap the end of a strand around the eye of the needle and pinch the wool as close to the needle as you can to make a sharp fold. This folded end of wool is then pushed through the needle's eye.

ADDITIONAL SUPPLIES

Graph paper is necessary for planning lettering. Paper with 10-to-the-inch grid lines is the most readily available and easiest to use. But you do not need paper with 12 grids to the inch for work on a 12-mesh canvas; 10 will do. As long as you use the same number of graph paper grids as you use canvas threads, it does not matter if they are not the same gauge. Albanene is a lovely, heavy tracing paper that can be obtained in art or architectural supply stores; it comes in a 10-to-the-inch grid and will take a great deal of erasing.

Tape for binding the raw edges of canvas to prevent raveling is available in needlepoint shops or art supply shops. Architect's masking tape in a 1-inch width is fine for this purpose.

Thimbles come in various sizes and should be tried on for a comfortable fit. They are easy to lose, so buy several at a time.

Scissors are a must for a needlepointer. You should have small snipping scissors for trimming the yarn ends and a large pair of shears for cutting canvas and hanks of yarn.

Proper **lighting** is as important as any tool. I prefer a Luxo Architect's Lamp, LC model, with both fluorescent and incandescent bulbs. The large fluorescent circle sheds a wide circle of light and is far easier on the eyes than a spotlight. The combination of two kinds of light is very much like daylight. You should position the light so that it casts no shadows on your work. Keep the light over your left shoulder if you are right-handed and over your right shoulder if you are left-handed.

PAINTS AND MARKERS

Acrylic paint with water as a medium, applied with fine sable brushes, was used for all these canvases. Liquitex is the brand name, and the paint comes in tubes or jars. Many people have had excellent results with **waterproof markers,** and some markers even state they are specifically for needlepoint. The main concern is blocking because during blocking, the canvas is drenched (perhaps even washed if that is necessary). Whatever coloring system you use, it *must* be waterproof. If you are uncertain, test a sample, especially if you are using markers.

Pencil is used to mark the working area on a bare canvas. Use a hard lead; 6H is good. Softer lead will be easily picked up by the yarn as you work and will discolor it. A kneaded rubber eraser will remove excess pencil marks.

READING GRAPHS AND DRAWINGS

Here are a few things to remember about reading the graphs in this book. The colors in the graphs are not meant to duplicate the colors of the finished items. In fact, they are intended to suggest other possible color combinations. In the graphs for the animals, the dark outline indicates where the background begins; the animal is left white. The graphs for the "Bon Appétit Chair Cushions" are done in the same way; the background is filled in, and the animal is outlined to show where the background begins.

I hope that you will use the graphs and drawings in this book with a free hand, substituting, adding, subtracting, and reconstructing to suit your needs. However, if you are new to working with graphed designs and find the task of counting difficult, you can follow the mesh size of the original; your finished piece will then measure about the same size as the original. Some of the items have a few rows of needlepoint added for extra background or seam allowance, so be sure to allow generous margins for this when you cut your canvas.

To determine how many inches of needlepoint a graph makes, count the number of design boxes across the width; then divide this number (which represents the number of canvas threads) by the mesh size, and you will know how many inches wide the design will be.

The size of a graphed needlepointed design is determined by the mesh size. If you want to change the size of the design, change the size of the mesh. Each box of color on the graph represents a stitch or the intersection of a vertical and a horizontal canvas thread. If there are 120 boxes of color across a row, there will be 120 stitches; therefore, if you use 10-to-the-inch canvas (120 stitches divided by 10 stitches), the piece will be 12 inches wide. But if you use a 12-to-the-inch canvas, the same 120 stitches across the graph (and therefore across the canvas) will make a piece 10 inches wide. A 14-mesh canvas with 120 stitches across will make a piece $8^4/_7$ inches (or about 8½ inches) wide.

If you are working from a drawing, you can make your needlepoint any size by having the design blown up or reduced in size by commercial photostat. Make a careful, simplified tracing of the photostat with a fine felt-tipped black marker, with heavier lines indicating the outer edges. Do this on tracing paper first, and then transfer it to the canvas.

FIGURING THE SIZE OF THE CUT CANVAS

Allow a 2-inch margin around the area to be needlepointed. This margin, which is left bare, will be needed to pull on when the piece is blocked. (If you intend to expand your design, allow more than 2 inches.) In addition, add three extra rows of stitches around the finished work for seam allowance if the item is to be sewn. Add two extra rows of stitches all around for a framed item, and add enough rows of the stitches to cover the width of the plywood, probably ½ inch for a plaque. Have the upholsterer who will finish the chair seat or pad draw a paper pattern so that you can mark the needlepoint area he needs on your canvas.

Here, for example, is a formula for cutting canvas for a 14-inch-square pillow. Reading from the left edge of the canvas, you will need 2 inches for margin, plus three rows for seam allowance, plus 14 inches for the needlepoint design, plus three rows for seam allowance, plus 2 inches for margin, which equals 18 inches and six rows of seam allowance. This is the width and length of the cut canvas. Mark the cutting lines in both directions by dragging a pencil between the canvas threads. Cut and bind the canvas. Then mark the outer edge of the needlepoint area by dragging the pencil between the canvas threads. Mark the centers of these lines; they will correspond to center lines of the graphs and drawings. Use a marking pen to mark the top binding.

PUTTING A DESIGN ON CANVAS

To put a **graphed** design on canvas, locate the center lines on the graph and on the canvas. Use as many guidelines on the canvas as you need. Paint or mark the canvas at the corners and the center. It is easier to transfer the design onto the canvas before stitching because then you don't have to concentrate on the graph and you can devote yourself to the pleasure of stitching. However, you can work directly from the graph to the bare canvas.

To put a **drawn** design on canvas, trace the drawing onto tracing paper with a fine black marking pen. Place the traced drawing on a covered flat surface such as a tabletop and tape it down. Put the prepared canvas over the drawing and tack it down; then paint the design in colors that correspond to the wools you have selected.

If you are using both a graph and a drawing, paint in the drawn design first and then the graphed frame, making sure it is placed evenly. Lettering is painted in last.

FINISHING

After you have finished your needlepoint, examine the canvas for missed stitches. To do this, hold the work up to a light. Light will gleam through the openings where stitches have been missed. You can also scan the work carefully with a magnifying glass. Now your needlepoint is ready for **blocking**. If it needs to be cleaned before it is mounted, wash it with a special mild wool soap according to the package instructions.

To block the canvas, wet it thoroughly by rolling it in a wrung-out bath towel. Cover a clean, flat board with brown wrapping paper. Again, using a 6H pencil, draw the shape of the finished needlepoint on the paper. Place the needlepoint face down on the paper, and tack it down, pulling on each side until it is the desired size and shape. Use rustproof tacks; ⅝-inch aluminum pushpins are excellent. Dry for at least twenty-four hours. If the canvas is very distorted, you may have to repeat this process.

An upholsterer will block needlepoint before he mounts a pillow, chair pad, or cover. He will also block a canvas so that you can take it to a frame shop. Unframed pictures can be treated as soft hangings or as plaques mounted over plywood.

A **plaque** is a mounted, unframed picture. A piece of ½-inch-thick plywood is cut to the size of the finished needlepoint design. A plaque design should include four needlepointed flaps, one along each edge. These will be folded back to cover the thickness of the plywood. Extra needlepoint, about ¼ by ¼ inch, is added at the four corners so that when the flaps are mitered to cover the sides, there is some extra needlepoint to ease around the corners and make them neat.

To cover the plywood, miter the corners of the finished piece, and tack the sides of the needlepoint along the thickness of the wood with ⅝-inch aluminum pushpins. (This is a temporary measure.) Then, put the plaque face down, and staple the canvas to the wood, using a heavy staple gun. If you do not have a staple gun, you can use small upholsterer's tacks. Now, remove the temporary side tacks. Cut away any extra canvas from the back. Cover the back with a square of felt, which can be glued in place. This method was used for the "Calendar of Flowers" and "Bon Appétit" plaques.

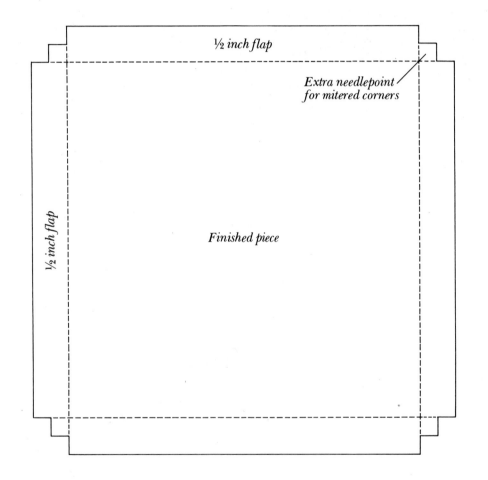

½ inch flap

Extra needlepoint
for mitered corners

½ inch flap

Finished piece

STITCHES AND STITCH VOCABULARY

Needlepoint is a system for embroidering an even, open mesh or canvas. The most frequently used stitch is **Tent,** which slants across the single intersection of a vertical and a horizontal canvas thread at 45-degree angle. When this slanted stitch covers more than one intersection, it is called **Slanted Gobelin.** When a straight stitch covers one or more canvas threads, it is called a **Straight Gobelin.** These are the basic needlepoint stitches; all other stitches are combinations, variations, or arrangements.

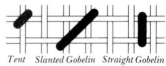

Tent   Slanted Gobelin   Straight Gobelin

In a **stitch sampler,** the display of stitches is as important as the design itself. A sampler is a very stimulating project because it is a challenge to work the design elements in different stitches and their variations. In the "American Primitive Sampler," I deliberately confined myself to most of the stitches that make up this basic stitch vocabulary. Inventing the new variations described here was a source of great pleasure. Kalem, for example, was worked in every possible combination of canvas threads. In the process, I realized that Kalem could be stitched slanting all to the right or all to the left. I used this new variation (one-way Kalem) for the robins' backs and the nest. Rep is another stitch that I have put to much use by varying its size and direction.

Compensating stitches are used in tight corners. Often, the shape of a design will not allow you to complete all the steps of a stitch pattern. Complete as much of the pattern as there are available canvas threads. Then, use compensating stitches to cover any remaining threads.

Sometimes, you will be able to anticipate the need for a compensating stitch. On those occasions, take an extra-large stitch to cover the canvas, rather than a small stitch. This is an **anticipated compensating stitch.**

Petit stitches are miniature stitches taken over the individual threads of Penelope canvas. Because the "American Primitive Sampler" was worked on Penelope, it was easy to change from full-sized to petit stitches.

Groundings are various small stitches that are easily maneuvered around design elements to create a textured background. Care should be taken to select a grounding that will complement the design, not distract the eye from it. Recommended groundings for the designs in this book include Cross, Diagonal Mosaic, Mosaic Chequer, Continuous Mosaic, and Rep.

Distortion (misshaping of canvas) is a source of annoyance to most needlepointers. It can be reduced somewhat by using an easy stitching tension and employing a diagonal method of working the rows wherever possible. Careful blocking will straighten some canvases, but a second blocking is often required because a straightened canvas that has not been mounted will pull back to its misshapen condition. This is the reason most of the lovely old pieces exhibited in museums are distorted.

In the course of working with a variety of stitches, I have noticed that stitches which are crossed in any way do not distort the canvas. The threads of the canvas are pulled in two directions by the crossing of the yarn and are thus kept straight through counterbalancing. For this reason, I have included in this stitch vocabulary, methods for crossing on the back of the canvas and extra crossing on the front of the canvas for accents. Try this two-way-stretch method. I think it will go a long way toward solving the distortion problem.

Grin through occurs when canvas threads peek out between stitches. This is sometimes caused by using yarn that is too thin. But some stitches will create grin through regardless of yarn thickness. A Backstitch made over these threads, either in a matching color or in a contrasting color to enhance the stitch, will eliminate this problem. Painting a canvas will also hide much grin through.

All needlepoint stitches begin at the back of the canvas (position 1 in the diagrams). The thread is brought through to the front of the canvas, and the needle is then inserted into the front of the canvas (position 2). In all the diagrams, the *odd* numbers indicate that the needle is coming up from the *back* of the canvas, and the *even* numbers indicate that the needle is going down through the *front* of the canvas.

STITCHES

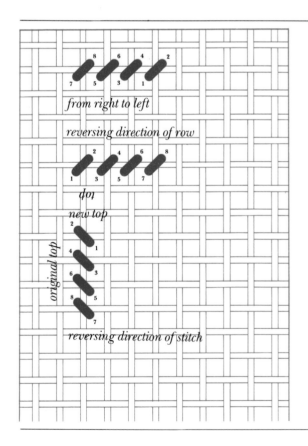

from right to left

reversing direction of row

top

new top

original top

reversing direction of stitch

A horizontal row of **Tent** is stitched from right to left.

When the row is finished, the canvas must be turned upside down in order to ensure that all stitches slant in the same direction.

To reverse the direction of the *stitch* from a slant to the right to a slant to the left, the canvas is given a quarter turn. Tent can be worked in a horizontal or vertical row.

Note to left-handed stitchers: If you stitch left-handed, the Tent will slant in the opposite direction from that shown in the first diagram. If you do not want to change your method but want a stitch that slants to the right, give your canvas a quarter turn, and proceed with your stitching. When the canvas is returned to its original position, the stitches will appear to have been worked right-handed.

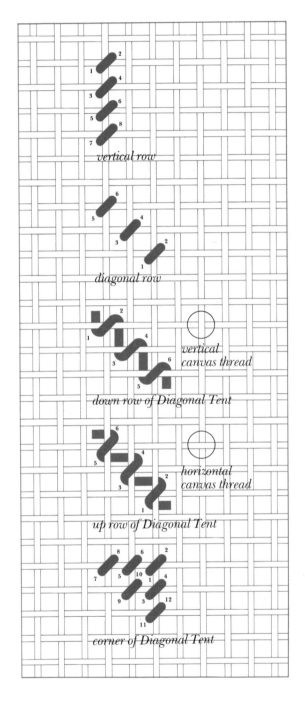

vertical row

diagonal row

vertical canvas thread

down row of Diagonal Tent

horizontal canvas thread

up row of Diagonal Tent

corner of Diagonal Tent

A vertical row of Tent is stitched from the *top* down. The canvas must be turned upside down for each row to make sure that the stitches in the next row slant in the same direction.

Tent should be stitched in diagonal rows whenever possible to minimize canvas distortion. **Diagonal Tent** is often called *Basketweave* because the stitches form a basketweave on the back of the work.

Down rows of Diagonal Tent are stitched over *vertical* canvas threads. The needle is held *vertically* and goes under two horizontal canvas threads as it descends.

Up rows of Diagonal Tent are stitched over *horizontal* canvas threads. The needle is held *horizontally* and goes under two vertical canvas threads as it ascends.

Consecutive rows of Diagonal Tent are made ascending and descending within a color area. At a straight edge, the first stitch of a row is made beside or under the last stitch of the preceding row.

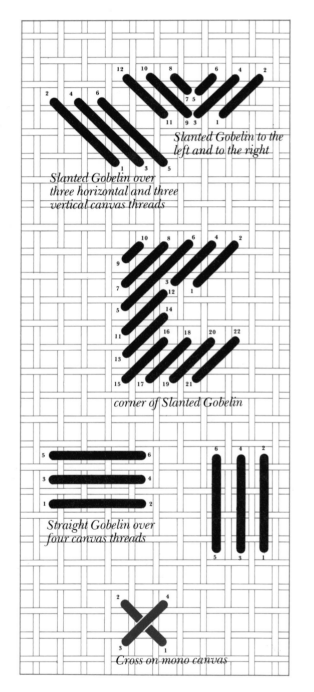

Slanted Gobelin is stitched over any combination of canvas threads. It can be slanted to the left or the right and can be worked in horizontal or vertical rows. In much of the lettering used in the designs in this book and in the "Libra Picture," Slanted Gobelin covers many different numbers of canvas threads.

Slanted Gobelin to the left and to the right

Slanted Gobelin over three horizontal and three vertical canvas threads

Slanted Gobelin can turn a corner neatly. A larger stitch is made as the corner is approached in order to avoid an awkward compensating stitch. (See the Greek key border of the "Needlework Box" for an example of turning a corner.)

corner of Slanted Gobelin

Straight Gobelin is stitched in horizontal or vertical rows over any consistent number of canvas threads. (See the straight sides of the octagon border in the "American Eagle Pillow" for an example of Straight Gobelin over four canvas threads.)

Straight Gobelin over four canvas threads

Cross is stitched on mono canvas by crossing a Slanted Gobelin to the left with a Slanted Gobelin to the right. It can be worked in horizontal or vertical rows. Good grounding.

Cross on mono canvas

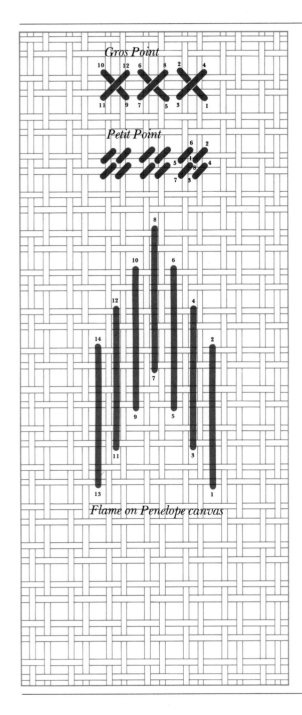

Gros Point

Petit Point

Flame on Penelope canvas

Gros Point is Cross stitched on Penelope canvas, where two closely woven vertical canvas threads cross two closely woven horizontal canvas threads. Gros Point is most often used with Petit Point.

Petit Point is Tent over the individual threads of Penelope canvas. (See the "Endless Knot Wedding Picture" and the lettering in the "American Primitive Sampler" for examples of Gros Point and Petit Point used together.)

Florentine, or **Flame,** is Straight Gobelin stitched in a diagonal row that rises or falls over a constant number of canvas threads. It can be stitched on a Penelope canvas splitting apart the vertical canvas threads and treating the double horizontal canvas threads as a single canvas thread to achieve a more flame like effect. (See the flames in the fireplace of the "American Primitive Sampler" for an example of Florentine worked on Penelope canvas between the closely woven vertical canvas threads.)

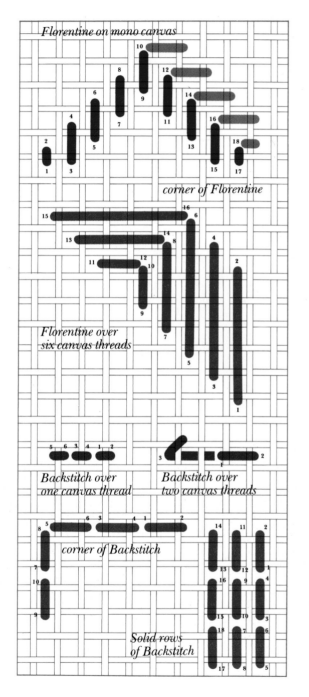

Florentine on mono canvas

corner of Florentine

Florentine over six canvas threads

Backstitch over one canvas thread

Backstitch over two canvas threads

corner of Backstitch

Solid rows of Backstitch

Florentine can be stitched over two or more canvas threads. Note the compensating stitch over one canvas thread at the straight edge. (See the "Needlework Box" for an example of Florentine over two canvas threads and with changes in direction.)

The direction of Florentine can be changed from vertical to horizontal. Compensating Straight Gobelins are made to cover the vacant canvas threads. (See the diagonal sides of the octagon border in the "American Eagle Pillow" for an example of Florentine over six canvas threads.)

Backstitch is made over one or two canvas threads, usually to cover grin through. Backstitch makes a long stitch on the back of the canvas but a short stitch on the front. This short stitch *always* goes back on itself. It can be worked in horizontal or vertical rows. Backstitch can also be used as a filling stitch in small areas. If worked in contrasting colors, it adds decoration. (See the vertical stripe in the blue wallpaper of the "American Primitive Sampler" for an example of solid rows of Backstitch.)

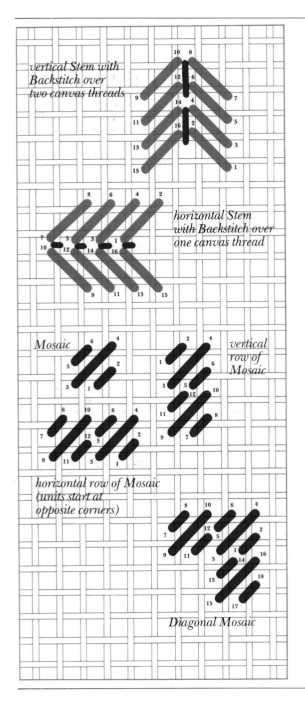

vertical Stem with
Backstitch over
two canvas threads

horizontal Stem
with Backstitch over
one canvas thread

Mosaic

vertical
row of
Mosaic

horizontal row of Mosaic
(units start at
opposite corners)

Diagonal Mosaic

Stem is composed of two rows of Slanted Gobelin that slant in opposite directions. It can be worked vertically or horizontally. The exposed canvas threads where the rows meet are covered with Backstitch, generally in a contrasting color. (See the red dividers in the "American Primitive Sampler" for an example of Stem.)

Mosaic is a square unit composed of three stitches. It starts in one corner with a Tent, has a Slanted Gobelin in the center, and ends with another Tent in the opposite corner. Mosaic can be stitched in horizontal or vertical rows, but it will distort the canvas. To avoid distortion, start the first unit with a Tent at the base and the next unit with a Tent at the top, alternating until the row is completed. If more than one row is required, use Diagonal Mosaic.

Diagonal Mosaic is Mosaic worked in diagonal rows. Because Tent is an integral part of each unit, Diagonal Mosaic fits easily around any Tent design. A Tent compensating stitch will fill in the extra bare threads. Maintaining loose tension will help avoid canvas distortion. Good grounding. (See the background in the "Sagittarius Pillow" for an example of Diagonal Mosaic.)

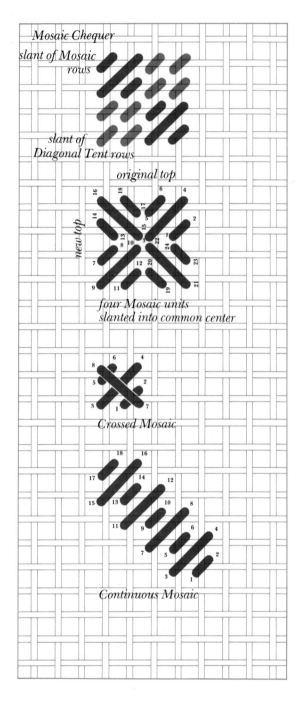

Mosaic Chequer

slant of Mosaic rows

slant of Diagonal Tent rows

original top

new top

four Mosaic units slanted into common center

Crossed Mosaic

Continuous Mosaic

Mosaic Chequer
Alternate Mosaic with a four-stitch unit of Diagonal Tent. Stitch the Mosaic in diagonal rows that slant upper left to lower right; stitch the Diagonal Tent units in diagonal rows that slant upper right to lower left. Use of two colors emphasizes the check design. Good grounding. (See the forelegs and front torso of the archer in the "Sagittarius Pillow" for an example of Mosaic Chequer.)

Four Mosaic units slanted into a common center creates a geometric flower. Work the two units that slant in the same direction first; then give the canvas a quarter turn and stitch the other two units.

Crossed Mosaic is Mosaic crossed to create a heavier texture. The crossing also prevents distortion. Crossed Mosaic can be alternated with Mosaic and worked in two colors for a pleasing texture. (See the sun in the "American Primitive Sampler" for an example of Crossed Mosaic.)

Continuous Mosaic alternates a Tent with a Slanted Gobelin (over two vertical and two horizontal canvas threads) and must be stitched in a diagonal row.

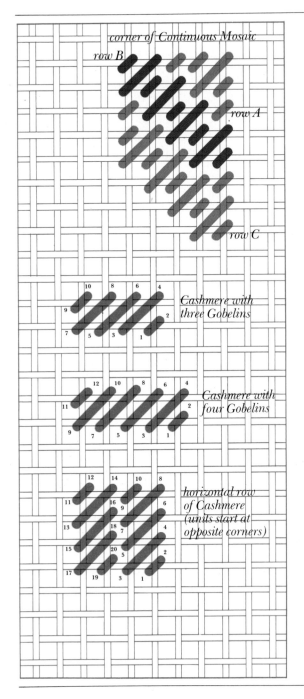

corner of Continuous Mosaic

row B

row A

row C

10 8 6 4

9   2

7 5 3 1

Cashmere with three Gobelins

12 10 8 6 4

11   2

9 7 5 3 1

Cashmere with four Gobelins

12 14 10 8

11   16   6
        9

13   18   4
        7

15   20   2
        5

17 19 3 1

horizontal row of Cashmere (units start at opposite corners)

Tent is used for compensating stitches at straight edges. All straight edges develop a consistent pattern of one Slanted Gobelin and two Tents. Good grounding.

Notice the diagonal row that slants upper right to lower left. A Slanted Gobelin alternates with a Tent in this direction just as it does in the direction in which the row is actually worked (upper left to lower right). This will help you to remember which stitch to make next. (See the backgrounds of the "Taurus," "Virgo," and "Leo" pillows for examples of Continuous Mosaic.)

Cashmere is a rectangular unit of four or more stitches. It starts in one corner with a Tent, has several Slanted Gobelins over two canvas threads, and finishes with another Tent in the opposite corner. Cashmere can be worked in horizontal or vertical rows, but it will distort the canvas. To avoid distortion, start the first unit with a Tent at the base and the next unit with a Tent at the top, alternating until the row is completed. (See the fireplace and the chimney in the "American Primitive Sampler" for examples of Cashmere.)

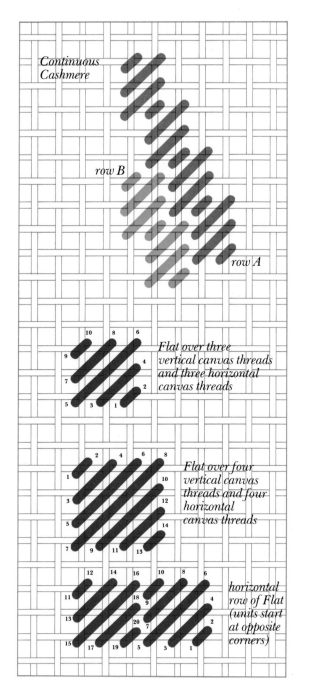

Continuous Cashmere

row B

row A

Flat over three vertical canvas threads and three horizontal canvas threads

Flat over four vertical canvas threads and four horizontal canvas threads

horizontal row of Flat (units start at opposite corners)

Continuous Cashmere alternates one Tent and two Slanted Gobelins (over two vertical and two horizontal canvas threads) and must be stitched in a diagonal row. Tent can be used for compensating stitches at the straight edges.

Notice that each row of Continuous Cashmere drops one horizontal canvas thread below the preceding diagonal row.

(See the legs of the water-bearer in the "Aquarius Picture" for an example of Continuous Cashmere.)

Flat is a square unit of five or more stitches. It consists of a Tent in one corner, three or more Slanted Gobelins in graduated lengths, and another Tent in the opposite corner. Flat can be stitched in horizontal or vertical rows, but it will distort the canvas. To avoid distortion, begin the first unit with a Tent at the base and the next unit with a Tent at the top, alternating until the row is completed. When more than one row of Flat is needed, stitch in diagonal rows. (See the harem pants in the "Virgo Pillow" for an example of Flat.)

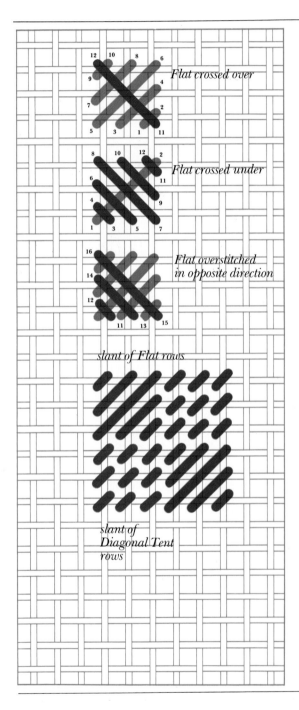

Flat crossed over

Flat crossed under

Flat overstitched in opposite direction

slant of Flat rows

slant of Diagonal Tent rows

Flat can be crossed over for another texture or crossed under for padding. The crossing also prevents distortion.

Flat can slant to the left or the right. It can also be stitched slanting in one direction and overstitched in the opposite direction.

(See the corners of the outer border in the "American Primitive Sampler" for an example of overstitched Flat.)

Flat Chequer alternates a Flat with a nine-stitch Diagonal Tent unit. Stitch the Flat in diagonal rows that slant upper left to lower right; stitch Diagonal Tent units in diagonal rows that slant upper right to lower left. Use of two colors accentuates the check effect.

(See the hearth in the "American Primitive Sampler" for an example of Flat Chequer.)

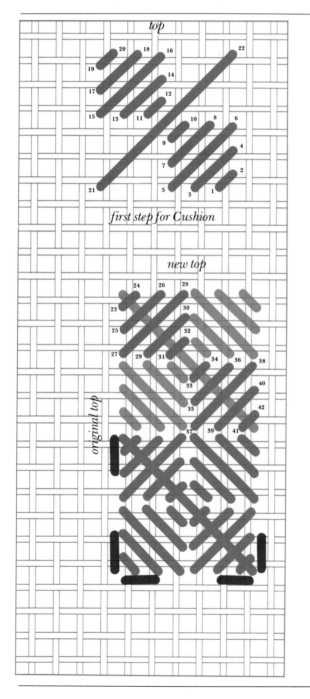

top

first step for Cushion

new top

original top

Cushion is a square unit composed of four Flats and one long Slanted Gobelin. The two Flat are stitched in a diagonal row with a long Slanted Gobelin between them. This long stitch bisects the completed square unit. The canvas is then given a quarter turn, and two Flats are stitched over the Slanted Gobelin. Cushion can be worked in vertical or horizontal rows. Backstitch may be added to cover grin through. (See the border in the "Bless This House Hanging" for an example of Cushion.)

Cushion Chequer can be made by alternating a Cushion and a square unit of thirty-six Tents. (See the floor pattern in entrance of the "American Primitive Sampler" for an example of Cushion Chequer.)

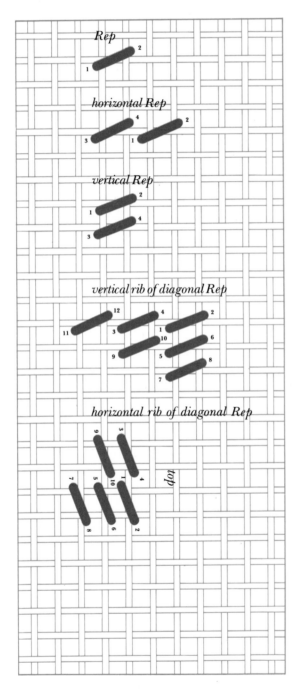

Rep is stitched over two vertical and one horizontal canvas threads. It can be stitched in horizontal and vertical rows, with each stitch made beside or under the last. For more than one row, Rep, like Diagonal Tent, should be worked in diagonal rows. And like Diagonal Tent, it will create a basketweave effect on the back. Rep makes a handsome vertically ribbed fabric. If a horizontal rib is desired, give the canvas a quarter turn before stitching. Good grounding.

(See the side panels in the "American Primitive Sampler" and the background in the "Rose Scroll Memory Book" for examples of Rep.)

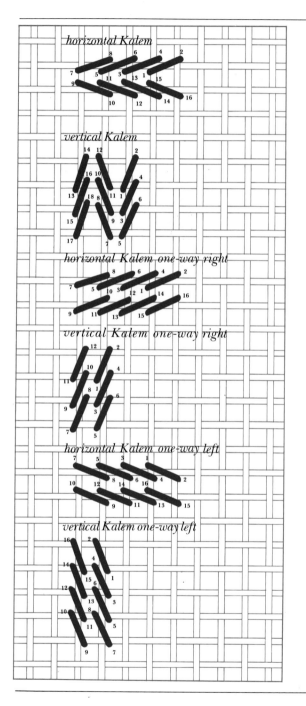

Kalem may be stitched in horizontal or vertical rows. Horizontal Kalem is stitched over one horizontal and two vertical canvas threads. Consecutive stitches overlap one vertical canvas thread. Each row slants in an opposite direction.

Vertical Kalem is stitched over one vertical and two horizontal canvas threads. Consecutive stitches overlap one horizontal canvas thread. Each row slants in an opposite direction.

(See the bow in the "Sagittarius Pillow" for an example of horizontal Kalem and the tail in that pillow for an example of vertical Kalem.)

All rows of horizontal Kalem one-way right are stitched in horizontal rows with stitches slanted to the right.

All rows of vertical Kalem one-way right are stitched in vertical rows with stitches slanted to the right.

All rows of horizontal Kalem one-way left are stitched in horizontal rows with stitches slanted to the left.

All rows of vertical Kalem one-way left are stitched in vertical rows with stitches slanted to the left. (See the "American Primitive Sampler" for all the varieties of Kalem.)

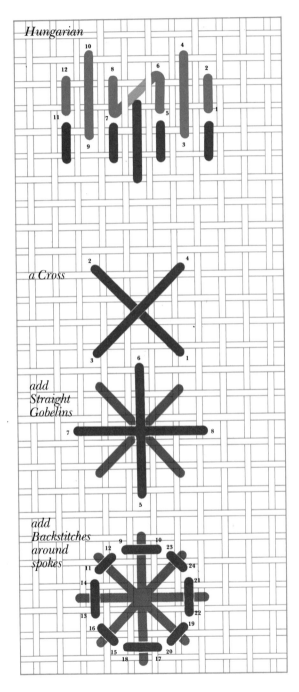

Hungarian is a unit of three Straight Gobelins worked horizontally. The first is stitched over two canvas threads; the second, over four; and the third, over two. Note that a space is left between the units. Hungarian is easily worked in rows of alternating colors. Stitch the first row in one color; stitch the next row in the second color, with the long center stitches of the units going into the vacant spaces between the units of the first row. Stitch the third row exactly the way you stitched the first and the fourth row exactly the way you stitched the second. (See the outer background of the "American Eagle Pillow" for an example of Hungarian.)

Asterisk (named for its resemblance to the printer's star) is a new stitch invented for this book. I believe that it enriches the language of needlepoint because that language contains very few round stitches. You can use Asterisk wherever a round accent is needed.

Asterisk starts with a Cross over four horizontal and four vertical canvas threads. Then, Straight Gobelins are made vertically and horizontally over six canvas threads at the center of the Cross. To complete the Asterisk, use Backstitches over the canvas threads around the outer spokes.

For fullest coverage of the canvas, work the Asterisk in two steps. Stitch the Cross only. Then, fill in the background surrounding the Cross. Complete the Asterisk by adding the Straight Gobelins and Backstitches, working over the area already stitched. (See the "Good Luck Pillow" and the door knob and curtain tiebacks in the "American Primitive Sampler" for examples of Asterisk.)

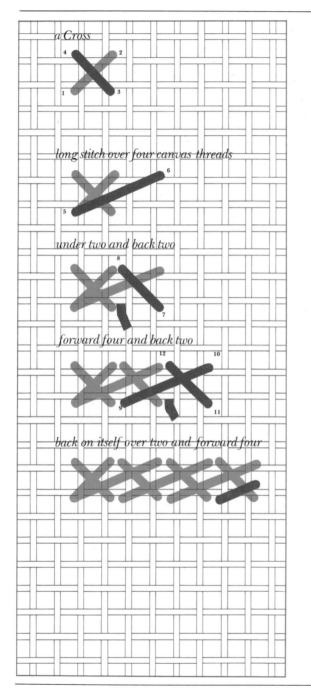

a Cross

long stitch over four canvas threads

under two and back two

forward four and back two

back on itself over two and forward four

Long-Armed Cross is worked across the canvas in one direction and the next row returns from the opposite direction, each row of stitching occupying two rows of canvas threads.

Always start the row with a Cross, the first half of which slants in the direction of the row. After the Cross is stitched, the row continues in the following way: forward over four vertical canvas threads, under two horizontal canvas threads and back over two vertical canvas threads, under two vertical canvas threads and forward over four. The rhythm of the stitch is always forward four and back two. The row can be ended with a compensating stitch.

(See the borders of the "Astrological Rug" for an example of Long-Armed Cross.)

STITCHING HINTS

Starting. There are two ways to start stitching. The simplest is to hold about an inch of yarn against the back of the canvas, in the direction of the stitching, and work the first five or six stitches over it. You can also start at the front of the work. Knot the end of the yarn, and insert the needle about an inch from the area the stitches are to cover. Work over the long stitch that this has formed on the back of the canvas. Cut away the knot on the front of the work as you approach it. This method is particularly helpful if you are using a frame.

Stopping. To end off a strand of yarn, weave it through five or six stitches on the back of the canvas, preferably within the color you are using. Try not to weave a dark color through a light color. It might show through or make the light color look dirty.

Where to begin. When you start work on a fresh canvas, it sometimes takes a little time before you are really "into" the design. I like to start a little to the left or right of the center of the canvas. That way, I can roll up or pin back the unworked areas. It is advisable to handle completed work as little as possible. Therefore, if you work out from the center, you will handle the outer areas less.

Stitch the details before you work the larger areas. Otherwise, you may not have enough canvas threads to do full justice to the complexities of your design.

It is also a good idea to work some of the background as you go along. That way, you will not be faced with large solid areas at the end. But when stitching some of the background before the design has been completed, you must remember that ultimately the stitches are going to meet and therefore must fit together perfectly, like parts of a puzzle. For this reason, stitch only those areas that connect with each other; do not skip all over the canvas. This is especially important when you are using any stitch other than Tent.

However, there is an exception to the details-first rule. When using a white or pale background, stitch the background first. If you are working with a graphed design, you can do this easily. Some colors, particularly reds and blues, seem to have hairs that are drawn into the light colors, producing color bleeding. One way of avoiding color bleeding is to find the *direction* of the yarn. If you hold a strand up to the light, you will see that the long hairs go in one direction. Draw the yarn between two fingers. It will feel smooth when you stroke it with the direction of the hairs, but it will burn your fingers when you stroke it in the opposite direction. Thread your needle with the hairs going away from the needle. If you do this, there will be fewer loose hairs bleeding into adjacent colors.

Twisted thread can be controlled if you give the needle a little turn in your sewing hand with each stitch. As you work, keep the yarn flat (with the plies beside each other) with the thumb of the hand that holds the canvas.

Ridges in Diagonal Tent are sometimes caused by working two successive rows up or down. The rows should alternate: one up, the next down. A tight tension or one that varies from row to row will also cause ridges. Try to match each stitch with its neighbor in the preceding row.

LETTERING
AND
ALPHABETS

The addition of a message and an inscription to a carefully chosen design creates a very special, very personal needlepoint celebration. Throughout this book, a wide variety of lettering styles has been worked in many different sizes.

Some of the graphs for alphabets and numbers are not included in this section because they are parts of other graphed designs. A script alphabet appears on the roof of the "American Primitive Sampler." The numbers 1 through 12 are graphed for the "Clock Pillow" and the "Twelve Days of Christmas Sock." There is an additional alphabet on the "ABC Appliqué Quilt" graph.

Often, graphed alphabets are very clear on paper but decrease in legibility when translated into needlepoint. All the alphabets in this book have been carefully designed specifically for needlepoint stitching, incorporating the slant of Tent or Gobelin in the direction of the shape of the letters. These alphabets are actually enhanced by the needlepoint stitching.

Two methods are used here for graphing alphabets. The first uses a box of color to represent each stitch. The second uses the grid lines of the graph paper to represent canvas threads; slanted lines at the intersections of the grid represent stitches. The second method is more suitable to the smaller letters because the stitches can be quickly counted for transfer to the canvas. And it makes it easier to visualize how long lines of lettering will look when stitched.

HOW TO USE THE LETTERING

1. Select the appropriate style and size of alphabet for your design.
2. Count the number of horizontal canvas threads required for the

height of the letters, and check that it will fit the desired location on the canvas.

3. On graph paper, mark off the number of vertical and horizontal canvas threads you can use for the entire lettered message.

4. If you wish to center a word or a single line of lettering, start with the middle letter of the middle word and work out toward either end. If you are using several lines of lettering, it is easier and neater to start all lines of words directly under each other at the left margin and leave an uneven margin on the right. The biography on the "American Primitive Sampler" is a good example.

5. Try to space the letters in each word so that they are pleasing to the eye. Some letters are quite open and do not need as much space around them as others do. Squint your eyes to see if you can get a feeling of even vertical lines within each word. The amount of spacing between words should be twice that between letters.

6. On scrap canvas the same gauge as the original, mark or paint the graphed lettering, making additional adjustments where they are needed.

7. Position the piece of scrap canvas over the site of the lettering. If you see that no further adjustments are needed, copy it onto the final canvas.

8. *A special note to left-handed needlepointers:* All the lettering in *Needlepoint Celebrations* has been designed with a 45-degree stitch slant to conform to the method used by a right-handed stitcher. Therefore, you should give the canvas a quarter turn before stitching in order to achieve the planned outline of the letters.

Bold Uppercase   over twenty-three canvas threads

Big Bold Uppercase over thirty-seven threads

Fractur Lowercase   over nine canvas threads

Tent Lowercase   over six canvas threads

Contemporary Uppercase	over seven canvas threads
Contemporary Uppercase	over six canvas threads
Contemporary Lowercase	over five canvas threads

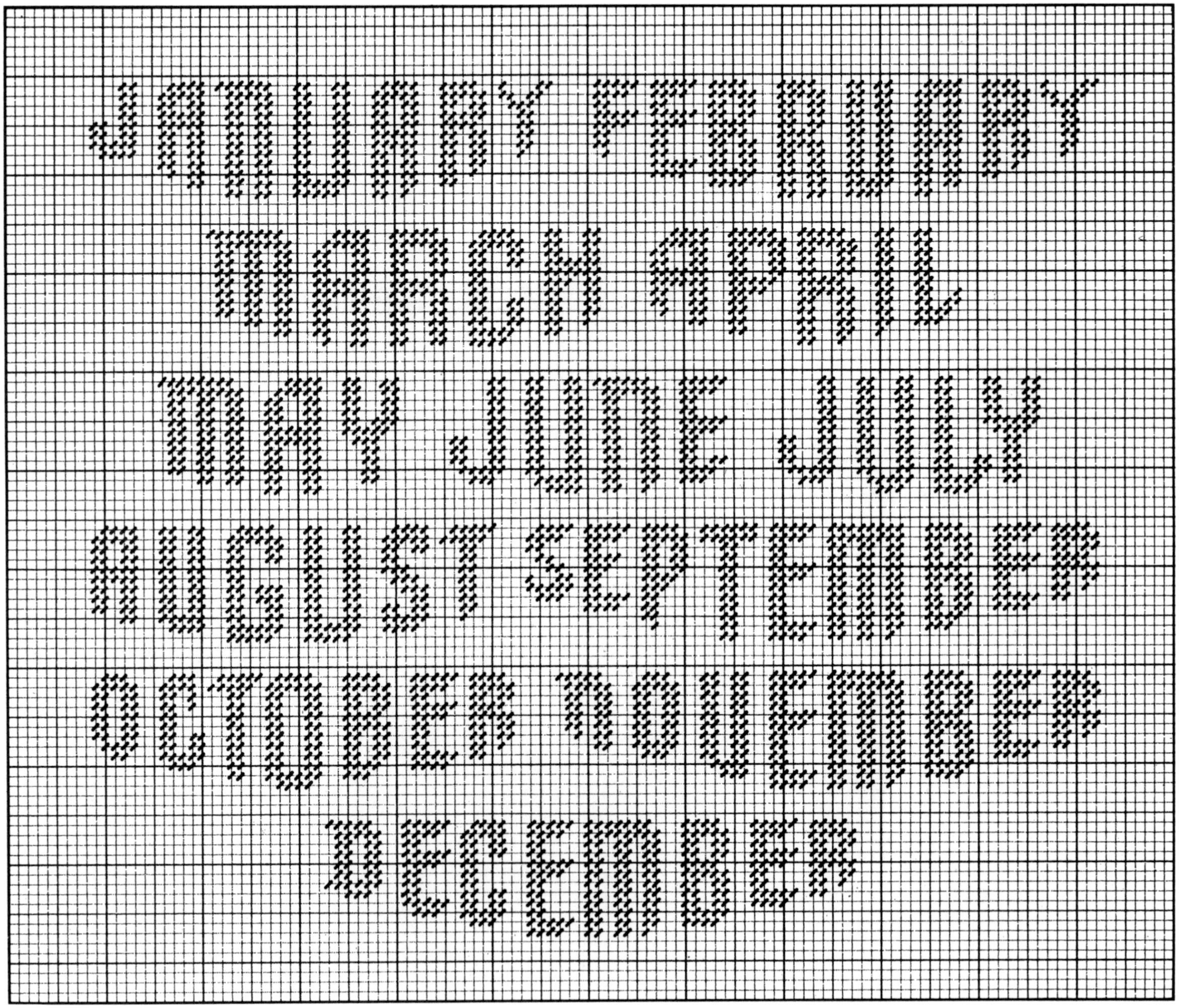

"Calendar of Flowers" month names

Fractur Uppercase   over twelve canvas threads

Tent Lowercase   over five canvas threads

APPENDIX

COLOR CHART

Note about purchasing yarn: Most yarn shops will not sell less than one ounce of yarn, so you will have to purchase more yarn than you need for some colors. Here are two recipes for estimating the total amount of yarn to purchase for a project. First, determine the number of square inches of needlepoint that there will be in the complete project.

For Persian, multiply the number of square inches by 1.5. You use 1.5 strands of Persian to the square inch for most stitches. There are 50 thirty-inch strands to the ounce. To convert to ounces of yarn needed, divide this number by 50.

For wool twist, multiply the number of square inches by 2. You use 2 strands of wool twist to the square inch for most stitches. There are 75 thirty-inch strands to the ounce. To convert to the number of ounces of yarn needed, divide this number by 75.

For a larger color area, try to estimate what percentage of the canvas is worked in that color. For example, a background may be 50 percent of your total canvas. You will need to buy half the estimated number of ounces for the background color.

Chinoiserie Anniversary Pillow

wool twist: Snowdrop (white background) 1/Malachite (exterior green background) 78

Persian: white 005/green 559

Au Ver A Soil Silk: light orange 621/dark orange 625/light pink 1014/dark pink 1015/yellow 2623/gold 536/tan 3813/brown 4516/light blue 112/dark blue 114

Endless Knot Wedding Picture

silk: pink 1015/light blue 112/dark blue 114/orange 625/green 245/champagne 3732

Good Luck Pillow

wool twist: Fiddlehead 82A/Heath 88
Persian: pink 850

Rose Scroll Memory Book

Persian: pinks 850, 855, 865/greens 577, G37/brown 172/blues 760, 765/white 012

Bless This House Hanging

Persian: blues, 750, 760/pink 860/red 845/greens 579, G54/golds 427, 445/ grays 162, 164, 166/rust 266/yellow 456

Pennsylvania German Fractur Birth Record

Persian: yellow gold 447/red 843/blue 342/green 527/brown 172/natural 496

January Pillow

Persian: Snowdrops and leaves: white 005/greens 553, 593. Daffodils and leaves: white 005/yellows 450, 458/coral 843/greens 512, 542. Background: gray 391. Border: white 005/coral 280

February Plaque

Persian: Primrose: gold 441/coral 260/greens 540, 545, 553. Peachblossom: corals 255, 260/gold 441/browns 131, 174/greens G54, G64. Background: blue 741. Border: yellow 452/blue 312

March Plaque

Persian: Violet: lavenders 650, 652/greens G54, G64. Tree Peony: reds 810, 855/gold 441/white 005/greens 540, 545. Background: yellow 452. Border: blues 312, 741

April Pillow

Persian: Daisy: white 005/greens 510, 574/gold 441/pink R70/greens G54, 505, 574. Anemone: reds R10, R70/gold 441/greens 505, 510, 555. Background: gold 438. Border: greens 510, 555

May Pillow

Persian: Iris: lavenders 621, 642/yellow 446/greens 510, 570. Hawthorn: roses 250,

254/blues 352, 367. Background: white 012. Border: green 570/rose 254

June Plaque

Persian: Honeysuckle: oranges 968, 988/greens 510, 570. Rose: roses 853, R80/greens 527, 566/yellow 446. Background: gold 531. Border: green 570/white 005

July Pillow

Persian: Lily: yellows 441, 456/greens 510, 574/orange 424. Water Lily: reds 865, R10, R70/greens 505, 510. Background: white 005. Border: greens 510, 555

August Pillow

Persian: Sunflower: golds 427, 447/brown 110/greens G54, G64. Lotus: lavenders 611, 650/blue 741/golds 427, 447/pinks 850, 860/greens 505, 545. Background: gold 437. Border: blue 741/gold 427

September Pillow

Persian: Mallow: pinks 828, 850, 860/golds 427, 437/greens 507, G54. Morning Glories: lavenders 611, 650/blues 741, 752/golds 427, 437/greens 507, 545. Background: gold 427. Border: lavender 611/gold 437

October Pillow

Persian: Carnation: pinks 845, 860, 870/greens 507, 591/white 005. Aster: lavenders 642, 650/yellows 447, 456/greens 559, 579. Background: gold 447. Border: greens 507, 591

November Plaque

Persian: Chrysanthemum: gold 441/white 005/brown 174/greens G54, G64. Camellia: pinks 855, R78/browns 131, 174/greens 545, 565. Background: blue 312. Border: yellow 452/blue 741

December Pillow

Persian: Holly: red 242/greens 507, 574. Poppy: red 242/pink R70/greens 524, 574. Background: white 005. Border: green 507/red 242

Aries Zodiac Rug

Persian: light gold 442/dark gold 440/coral 843

Taurus Pillow

Persian: peach 436/brown 140/beige 513/blue 742

Gemini Zodiac Rug

Persian: green 559/white 032/blue 310/

Cancer or the Moonchild Pillow

Persian: dark violet 640/light violet 650/green 574/magentas 644, 821/white 005

Leo Pillow

Persian: yellows 438, 441/coral 843/blue 365

Virgo Pillow

Persian: red violet 643/blue violet 611/green 545/peach 853/white 005/light blue B43

Libra Picture

Persian: blues 365, 386/white 005/orange 424

Scorpio Zodiac Rug

Persian: pale gold 438/coral 843/wine 236/blue 752

Sagittarius Pillow

Persian: mauve 229/white 005/orange 441/blues 742, 754, 793

Capricorn Pillow

Persian: blue-green 342/brown 172/gold 541

Aquarius Picture

Persian: turquoise 738/blue 312/coral 843/gold 015

Pisces Zodiac Rug

Persian: green 559/white 005/blue 741/gray 162

Zodiac Symbols
Aquarius, Gemini, Capricorn, Cancer

Persian: brown 113/rust 215/gold 445/white 005

Aries, Leo, Libra

Persian: white 005/turquoise 773/blue 310

Pisces, Scorpio, Virgo, Sagittarius

Persian: white 005/gold 440/blue 310/coral 849

Taurus

Persian: orange 424/beige 445/green 507

Clock Pillow

Persian: golds 015, 427, 453/reds 843, 853/greens 516, 546/blue 330/gray 164/white 012/browns 145, 462/black 050

American Primitive Sampler

silk: white and flesh
wool twist: Pennant Red 32/Lady Slipper Pink 41/Erin Green 85/Green Bottle 79/Irish Bell (light turquoise) 76/Atoll Green (dark turquoise) 74/Rust 20/Old Ivory 3/Coffee (dark brown) 100/Bayberry (light blue) 58/Delphinium (medium blue) 59/Mariner Blue (royal) 56/China Blue (navy) 52/Topaz (gold) 15A

Persian: yellow 442/rust 269

Provincial Birth Record

Persian: yellow 456/white 011/pink R70/blue 745/green 569/flesh 988/rust 416

Horn of Plenty Picture

Persian: white mat 005/neutral background 015/light gold 453/medium gold 445/dark gold 145. Pineapple: gold 441/green 553. Peaches: pale orange 454/yellow gold 427. Grapes: light lavender 650/medium lavender 652/dark lavender 642/light grape 620/medium grape 615/dark grape 610. Strawberries: pink 855/red 845. Leaves: light green 590/medium green 553/dark green 540/light blue 556/dark blue 522

Twelve Days of Christmas

wool twist: Malachite (green background) 78/Snowdrop 1/Magenta 38/New Leaf (light green) 83

Persian: orange 965/dull gold 427/bright yellow 452/flesh 265/turquoise 738/red violet 643/red R50/rusty brown 414

ABC Appliqué Quilt

Persian: dark blue 763/light blue 783/red 845/pink 860/orange 968/gold 440/green 555/purple 650/white 005

Open and Closed Sign
Persian: light blue 742/dark blue 733/light purple 650/dark purple 642/light gold 442/brown 145/light pink 855/red 850/light green 542/dark green 520/pale green 593

American Eagle Pillow

Persian: light blue 396/medium light blue 386/medium dark blue 330/navy blue 365/off white 012

Shop Sign

Persian: brown (background) 131/gold (background) 447/red (background) R50/off white (palette) 012/dark blue 743/light blue 733/red R50/pink R70/dark purple 650/light purple 652/green G64/dark gray 166/black 050

Needlework Box

Persian: navy 365/light blue 741/gold 427/white 032

Bon Appétit Chair Cushions or Plaques

wool twist: Chickory Blue (medium blue) 55/Bayberry (light blue) 58/Blue Ice (white) 53A

Persian: blue (background) 742/yellow 441/red 242/coral 852

The Naturalist Tapestry

Persian: leaf green 574/leaf green dark 510/light green (background) 592/medium green (ribbon border) 566/pink 831/rose light 288/rose medium 232/coral 852/yellow 442/gold 427/rust 215/blue 743

BIBLIOGRAPHY

Christensen, Erwin O. The Index of American Design. New York: Macmillan, 1950.

De Jonge, C.H. *Delft Ceramics.* New York: Praeger, 1970.

Groves, Sylvia. *The History of Needlework Tools.* London: Country Life Books, 1968.

Honour, Hugh. *Chinoiserie.* London: John Murray, 1973.

Jouets, Une selection du Musée de Sonneberg R.D.A. Paris: Musée Des Arts Décoratifs, Louvre, 1973.

Lehner, Ernst, and Lehner, Johanna. *Folklore and Symbolism of Flowers, Plants and Trees.* New York: Tudor, 1960.

Lipman, Jean, and Winchester, Alice. *The Flowering of American Folk Art.* New York: Viking in cooperation with the Whitney Museum, 1974.

Safford, Carleton L., and Bishop, Robert. *America's Quilts and Coverlets.* New York: Dutton, 1972.

Shahn, Ben. *A Partridge in a Pear Tree.* New York: Museum of Modern Art, 1959.

Staff, Frank. *The Valentine and Its Origin.* New York: Praeger, 1969.

Understanding Astrology. London: Octopus Books, 1973.

Wust, Klaus. *Virginia Fractur.* Edinburg, Shenandoah History, 1972.